DANTE GABRIEL ROSSETTI

Dante Gabriel Rossetti

John Nicoll

MACMILLAN PUBLISHING CO., INC.
New York

Macmillan Publishing Co., Inc.
866 Third Avenue, New York, N.Y. 10022

Library of Congress Cataloging in Publication Data

Nicoll, John.
    Dante Gabriel Rossetti.

      Bibliography: p.
      Includes index.
      1. Rossetti, Dante Gabriel, 1828-1882.
ND497.R8N52 1976   759.2 [B]   75-23267
ISBN 0-02-589340-8

First published in 1975 by Studio Vista,
an imprint of Cassell and Collier Macmillan Publishers Ltd
35 Red Lion Square, London WC1R 4SG
and at Sydney, Auckland, Toronto, Johannesburg
an affiliate of Macmillan Inc. New York

Designed by John Nicoll

First American Edition 1976

Printed in Great Britain

For my Father and Mother

Preface

This book does not aim to do more than present an interpretation of Rossetti's art within the broad context of the development of capitalism and romanticism in mid-nineteenth-century Britain. Brevity has meant that many of the suggestions and allusions have not been worked out and developed in detail, while other statements have perhaps been made with an unqualified bluntness that may provoke disagreement.

One of the main problems involved in approaching the history of art from a broadly Marxist perspective is the relatively undeveloped nature of the discipline. So that on the one hand it is easy to make unsupported and reductive assertions relating (for example) economic 'base' to artistic 'superstructure', while on the other it is equally easy to become involved in long excursuses on the exact significance of specific artistic, historical or economic developments. I have probably not escaped these dangers, but am only too aware of them. Nonetheless it seems to me to be an important and worthwhile task to try to use this particular approach to art at a relatively popular level.

Many people have helped me in the writing of the book by providing ideas, information, material and criticism. I am extremely grateful to them all and would like particularly to thank John Bryson, Maggie Cawkwell, John Fekete, Jo Hickey, Tristram Holland, Mary Lewis, Andrew Lincoln, David Phillips, Linda Smith and Virginia Surtees. I am grateful to the Paul Mellon Centre for Studies in British Art (London) for help with a photograph. Above all I am indebted to Frances, my wife, and to my parents for their continuous understanding, help and criticism. The shortcomings which remain are, of course, my own responsibility.

Tufnell Park
January 1975

Contents

List of plates   10

Chapter 1   17

Chapter 2   34

Chapter 3   66

Chapter 4   94

Chapter 5   134

Notes   166

Index   171

List of Plates

All paintings are oil on canvas or panel unless otherwise stated. Dimensions are in centimetres and inches, height preceding width.

COLOUR PLATES

1. *The Girlhood of Mary Virgin* 1849 81·9 × 65·4 cm. 32¼ × 25¾ in. Tate Gallery, London

2. *Ecce Ancilla Domini! (The Annunciation)* 1850 73 × 41·9 cm. 28⅝ × 16½ in. Tate Gallery, London

3. *Ruth and Boaz* 1855 Watercolour, 31·4 × 17·5 cm. 12⅜ × 6⅞ in. Private Collection

4. *Girl Singing to a Lute* 1853 Watercolour, 22·5 × 10·5 cm. 8⅞ × 4⅛ in. London Art Market 1973

5. D. G. Rossetti and Elizabeth Siddal *The Quest of the Holy Grail c.* 1855 Watercolour, 27·9 × 23·8 cm. 11 × 9⅜ in. Private Collection

6. *Carlisle Wall* 1853 Watercolour, 24·8 × 17·1 cm. 9¾ × 6¾ in. Ashmolean Museum, Oxford

7. *Dante's Vision of Rachel and Leah* 1855 Watercolour, 35·6 × 31·8 cm. 14 × 12½ in. Tate Gallery, London

8. *Found* 1854-81 91·4 × 80 cm. 36 × 31½ in. Wilmington Society of Fine Arts (Bancroft Collection), Wilmington, Delaware

9. *Arthur's Tomb* 1855 Watercolour, 22·9 × 36·8 cm. 9 × 14½ in. Private Collection

10. *Sir Launcelot's Vision of the Sanc Grael* 1857 Watercolour, 67·9 × 103·5 cm. 26¾ × 40¾ in. Ashmolean Museum, Oxford

11. *How Sir Galahad, Sir Bors and Sir Percival were fed with the Sanc Grael; but Sir Percival's sister Died by the Way* 1864 Watercolour, 29·2 × 41·9 cm. 11½ × 16½ in. Tate Gallery, London

12. *The Tune of Seven Towers* 1857 Watercolour, 32·4 × 36·5 cm. 12⅜ × 14⅜ in. Tate Gallery, London

13. *The Chapel before the Lists* 1857 Watercolour, 39·4 × 41·3 cm. 15½ × 16¼ in. Tate Gallery, London

14. *St Catherine* 1857 34·3 × 24·1 cm. 13½ × 9½ in. Tate Gallery, London

15. *Before the Battle* 1858 Watercolour, 42·2 × 27·9 cm. 16⅝ × 11 in. Museum of Fine Arts, Boston, Mass.

16. *Sir Galahad at the Ruined Chapel* 1859 Watercolour, 29·2 × 34·3 cm. 11½ × 13½ in. City Museum and Art Gallery, Birmingham

17. *The Seed of David* (central panel) 1858-64 228·6 × 152·4 cm. 90 × 60 in. Cathedral, Llandaff

18. *Beata Beatrix* 1864 86·4 × 66 cm. 34 × 26 in. Tate Gallery, London

19. *The Merciless Lady* 1865 Watercolour, 31·1 × 31·4 cm. 12¼ × 12⅜ in. Private Collection

20. *The Beloved* 1865-6 82·6 × 76·2 cm. 32½ × 30 in. Tate Gallery, London

21. *Monna Vanna* 1866 88·9 × 86·4 cm. 35 × 34 in. Tate Galley, London

22. *La Pia de' Tolomei* 1868-80 105·4 × 120·6 cm. 41½ × 47½ in. Museum of Art, University of Kansas, Lawrence, Kansas

23. *Mariana* 1870 109·2 × 88·9 cm. 43 × 35 in. Art Gallery and Regional Museum, Aberdeen

24. *Dante's Dream at the Time of the Death of Beatrice* 1856 Watercolour, 47 × 65·4 cm. 18½ × 25¾ in. Tate Gallery, London

25. *Dante's Dream at the Time of the Death of Beatrice* 1871 210·8 × 317·5 cm. 83 × 125 in. Walker Art Gallery, Liverpool

26. *Proserpine* 1877 116·8 × 55·8 cm. 46 × 22 in. Private Collection

27. *La Ghirlandata* 1873 115·6 × 87·6 cm. 45½ × 34½ in. Guildhall Art Gallery, London

BLACK AND WHITE PLATES

1. *Gabriele Rossetti* 1853 Pencil, 27 × 20·6 cm. 10⅝ × 8⅛ in. Private Collection

2. *Self Portrait* 1847 Pencil, 19 × 19·7 cm. 7½ × 7¾ in. National Portrait Gallery, London

3. *Ford Madox Brown* 1852 Pencil, 16·5 × 11.4 cm. 6½ × 4½ in. National Portrait Gallery, London

4. Ford Madox Brown *John Wycliffe Reading his Translation of the Bible to John of Gaunt in the Presence of Chaucer and Gower* 1848 120·6 × 153·7 cm. 47½ × 60½ in. City Art Gallery, Bradford

5. *Angels Watching over the Crown of Thorns* 1848 49·5 × 34·3 cm. 19½ × 13½ in. Private Collection

6. *Bottles* 1848 37·5 × 34·9 cm. 14¾ × 13¾ in. Wilmington Society of Fine Arts (Bancroft Collection), Wilmington, Delaware

7. William Holman Hunt *The Eve of St Agnes* 1848 77·5 × 113 cm. 30½ × 44½ in. Guildhall Art Gallery, London

8. *Faust—Gretchen and Mephistopheles in the Church* 1848 Pen and ink, 32·4 × 17·8 cm. 12¾ × 7 in. Private Collection

9. *Faust—Gretchen and Mephistopheles in the Church* 1848 Pen and ink, 27·3 × 20·6 cm. 10¾ × 8⅛ in. Private Collection

10. *Genevieve* 1848 Pen and ink, 27·3 × 14 cm. 10¾ × 5½ in. Fitzwilliam Museum, Cambridge

11. *Ululame c.*1848 Pen and ink over pencil, 20·6 × 19·7 cm. 8⅛ × 7¾ in. City Museum and Art Gallery, Birmingham

12. *The Sleeper c.* 1847 Pen and ink, 22·9 × 12 cm. 9 × 4¾ in. British Museum, London

13. *The Raven* c. 1847 Pen and wash, 22·9 × 21·6 cm. 9 × $8\frac{1}{2}$ in. Victoria and Albert Museum, London

14. William Etty *The Judgement of Paris* 1826 177·8 × 272·9 cm. 70 × $107\frac{1}{2}$ in. Lady Lever Art Gallery, Port Sunlight

15. Sir David Wilkie *The Irish Whiskey Still* 1840 119·4 × 157·5 cm. 47 × 62 in. National Galleries of Scotland, Edinburgh

16. Alfred Elmore *The Origin of the Stocking Frame* 1847 80 × 106·7 cm. $31\frac{1}{2}$ × 42 in. Castle Museum and Art Gallery, Nottingham

17. Richard Redgrave *The Poor Teacher* 1844 71·1 × 91·4 cm. 28 × 36 in. Victoria and Albert Museum, London

18. William Mulready *The Sonnet* 1839 35·6 × 30·5 cm. 14 × 12 in. Victoria and Albert Museum, London

19. William Dyce *Virgin and Child* 1838 75·6 × 52 cm. $29\frac{3}{4}$ × $20\frac{1}{2}$ in. Castle Museum and Art Gallery, Nottingham

20. William Dyce *Christabel* 1855 50·8 × 43·2 cm. 20 × 17 in. Museum and Art Gallery, Glasgow

21. *Dante Drawing an Angel on the First Anniversary of the Death of Beatrice* 1848 Pen and ink and pencil, 27·9 × 23·2 cm. 11 × $9\frac{1}{8}$ in. Royal Institute of British Architects, London

22. *Dante Drawing an Angel on the First Anniversary of the Death of Beatrice* 1849 Pen and ink, 40 × 32·7 cm. $15\frac{3}{4}$ × $12\frac{7}{8}$ in. City Museum and Art Gallery, Birmingham

23. William Holman Hunt *Valentine Rescuing Sylvia from Proteus* 1851 98·4 × 133·4 cm. $38\frac{3}{4}$ × $52\frac{1}{2}$ in. City Museum and Art Gallery, Birmingham

24. *The Bower Meadow* 1850-72 85 × 67·3 cm. $33\frac{1}{2}$ × $26\frac{1}{2}$ in. City Art Gallery, Manchester

25. *The Passover in the Holy Family—Gathering Bitter Herbs* 1855-6 Watercolour, 40·7 × 43·2 cm. 16 × 17 in. Tate Gallery, London

26. *Mary in the House of St John* 1858 Watercolour, 45·7 × 35·6 cm. 18 × 14 in. Wilmington Society of Fine Arts, Wilmington, Delaware

27. *St John Comforting the Virgin at the Foot of the Cross* c. 1857-8 Pen and ink, 16·5 × 15·2 cm. $6\frac{1}{2}$ × 6 in. Fitzwilliam Museum, Cambridge

28. *The Annunciation* 1861 Watercolour, 60·3 × 25·4 cm. $25\frac{3}{4}$ × 10 in. Fitzwilliam Museum, Cambridge

29. *'Hist!' said Kate the Queen* 1851 32·4 × 59·7 cm. $12\frac{3}{4}$ × $23\frac{1}{2}$ in. Eton College

30. *The Laboratory* 1849 Watercolour, 19·4 × 24·4 cm. $7\frac{5}{8}$ × $9\frac{5}{8}$ in. City Museum and Art Gallery, Birmingham

31. *The Damsel of the Sanct Grael* 1857 Watercolour, 35·2 × 11·7 cm. $13\frac{7}{8}$ × $4\frac{5}{8}$ in. Tate Gallery, London

Since the many portraits of Elizabeth Siddal are almost undatable on stylistic grounds, dates are only given for inscribed drawings.

32. *Elizabeth Siddal* Pencil, 12 × 11·4 cm. $4\frac{3}{4}$ × $4\frac{1}{2}$ in. Victoria and Albert Museum, London

33. *Elizabeth Siddal* 1854 Pen and ink, 22·2 × 9·8 cm. $8\frac{3}{4}$ × $3\frac{7}{8}$ in. Victoria and Albert Museum, London

34. *Elizabeth Siddal* 1854 Watercolour, 22·2 × 19·7 cm. $8\frac{1}{2}$ × $7\frac{3}{4}$ in. Private Collection

35. *Elizabeth Siddal* 1854 Pencil, 17·1 × 11·4 cm. $6\frac{3}{4}$ × $4\frac{1}{2}$ in. City Museum and Art Gallery, Birmingham

36. *Elizabeth Siddal* Pencil, 30·8 × 18·7 cm. $12\frac{1}{8}$ × $7\frac{3}{8}$ in. City Museum and Art Gallery, Leicester

37. *Elizabeth Siddal* 1854 Pencil, 34·6 × 16·2 cm. $13\frac{5}{8}$ × $6\frac{3}{8}$ in. City Museum and Art Gallery, Birmingham

38. *Elizabeth Siddal* Pen and ink and wash over pencil, 19 × 12 cm. $7\frac{1}{2}$ × $4\frac{3}{4}$ in. From the Makins Collection

39. *Elizabeth Siddal* 1852 Pencil, 19·4 × 12·7 cm. $7\frac{5}{8}$ × 5 in. Private Collection

40. *Elizabeth Siddal* Pen and wash, 19 × 12·7 cm. 7½ × 5 in. Private Collection

41. *Elizabeth Siddal* Pen and ink, 13 × 11·4 cm. 5⅛ × 4½ in. Ashmolean Museum, Oxford

42. *Elizabeth Siddal* 1850-65 Watercolour and Pencil, 33·7 × 22·9 cm. 13¼ × 9 in. Fitzwilliam Museum, Cambridge

43. *Elizabeth Siddal* Pencil, 25·7 × 25·4 cm. 10⅛ × 10 in. Fitzwilliam Museum, Cambridge

44. *D. G. Rossetti sitting to Elizabeth Siddal* 1853 Pen and ink, 10·8 × 16·5 cm. 4¼ × 6½ in. City Museum and Art Gallery, Birmingham

45. Elizabeth Siddal *Clerk Sanders* 1857 Watercolour, 28 × 19·7 cm. 11 × 7¾ in. Fitzwilliam Museum, Cambridge

46. *St Cecilia* 1856-7 Pen and ink, 33 × 17·8 cm. 13 × 7 in. City Museum and Art Gallery, Birmingham

47. Study for woodcut of *St Cecilia* 1856-7 Pen and ink, 12·7 × 10·2 cm. 5 × 4 in. Ashmolean Museum, Oxford

48. *Paolo and Francesca c.* 1855 Pencil, 22 × 17·1 cm. 8⅝ × 6¾ in. Private Collection

49. *The Ballad of Fair Annie c.*1855 Pen and wash, 33 × 17·8 cm. 13 × 7 in. British Museum, London

50. *La Belle Dame sans Merci c.*1855 Pencil, pen and wash, 33 × 17·8 cm. 13 × 7 in. British Museum, London

51. *Dante drawing an Angel on the First Anniversary of the Death of Beatrice* 1853 Watercolour, 42 × 61 cm. 16½ × 24 in. Ashmolean Museum, Oxford

52. Study for *Found* 1853 Pen and ink and wash, 21 × 18·4 cm. 8¼ × 7¼ in. British Museum, London

53. Study for *Found c.*1855 Pen and ink, 23·5 × 21·9 cm. 9¼ × 8⅝ in. City Museum and Art Gallery, Birmingham

54. & 55. Studies for *Found c.*1859-61 41·9 × 47 cm. 16½ × 18½ in. (overall dimensions of single panel on which both details are painted) Museum and Art Gallery, Carlisle

56. Study for *Found c.*1860 Pen and ink, 17·8 × 19·7 cm. 7 × 7¾ in. City Museum and Art Gallery, Birmingham

57. *Hesterna Rosa* 1853 Pen and sepia, 9·8 × 14 cm. 3⅞ × 5½ in. Private Collection

58. *The Gate of Memory c.*1857 Watercolour, 33·7 × 26·7 cm. 13¼ × 10½ in. Private Collection

59. *Algernon Charles Swinburne* 1861 Watercolour and pencil, 18·1 × 17·1 cm. 7⅛ × 6¾ in. Fitzwilliam Museum, Cambridge

60. Study for *Sir Launcelot's Vision of the Sanc Grael* 1857 Pen and ink and pencil, 25·1 × 31·8 cm. 9⅞ × 12½ in. City Museum and Art Gallery, Birmingham

61. Study for *Sir Launcelot's Vision of the Sanc Grael* 1857 Pen and ink and pencil, 22·2 × 11·4 cm. 8¾ × 4½ in. City Museum and Art Gallery, Birmingham

62. Study for *Sir Launcelot's Vision of the Sanc Grael* 1857 Pen and ink and pencil, 22·9 × 13·7 cm. 9 × 5⅜ in. Fitzwilliam Museum, Cambridge

63. Study for *The Attainment of the Sanc Grael* 1857 Pen and ink, 25·4 × 34·9 cm. 10 × 13¾ in. British Museum, London

64. *Jane Morris* 1857 Pencil, 47·6 × 33 cm. 18¾ × 13 in. Society of Antiquaries (Kelmscot Manor, Oxfordshire)

65. William Morris *Queen Guinevere* 1858 28½ × 19¾ in. Tate Gallery, London

66. *The Blue Closet* 1857 Watercolour, 34·3 × 24·8 cm. 13½ × 9¾ in. Tate Gallery, London

67. *The Wedding of St George and the Princess Sabra* 1857 Watercolour, 34·3 × 34·3 cm. 13½ × 13½ in. Tate Gallery, London

68. *A Christmas Carol* 1857-8 Watercolour, 33·7 × 29·2 cm. 13¼ × 11½ in. Fogg Art Museum, Harvard University, Greville L. Winthrop Bequest, Cambridge, Mass.

69. Study for *The Seed of David* c.1856 Watercolour, 40·6 × 29·2 cm. 16 × 11½ in. wings 27·9 × 12·7 cm. 11 × 5 in. Tate Gallery, London

70. Detail of Plate 69

71. Detail of Plate 69

72. Study for *The Seed of David* 1862 Pen and ink and pencil, 45·7 × 23·5 cm. 18 × 9¼ in. National Museum of Wales, Cardiff

73. *Sir Launcelot in the Queen's Chamber* 1857 Pen and ink, 26 × 34·9 cm. 10¼ × 13¾ in. City Museum and Art Gallery, Birmingham

74. *Mary Magdalene at the Door of Simon the Pharisee* 1858 Pen and ink and wash, 52·7 × 45·7 cm. 20¾ × 18 in. Fitzwilliam Museum, Cambridge

75. *Bocca Baciata* 1859 33·7 × 30·5 cm. 13¼ × 12 in. Private Collection

76. *St George and the Dragon* 1861-2 Pen, brush and ink, 49·5 × 62·2 cm. 19½ × 24½ in. City Museum and Art Gallery, Birmingham

77. *The Wedding of St George* 1864 Watercolour, 25·4 × 34·9 cm. 10 × 13¾ in. Private Collection

78. *Cassandra* 1861 Pen and ink, 33 × 47 cm. 13 × 18½ in. British Museum, London

79. *Dr Johnson at the Mitre* 1860 Pen and ink, 21·6 × 21 cm. 8½ × 8¼ in. Fitzwilliam Museum, Cambridge

80. *Writing on the Sand* c.1858 Pen and ink and pencil, 22·2 × 17·1 cm. 8¾ × 6¾ in. Private Collection

81. *How They Met Themselves* 1860 Pen and ink and wash, 27 × 21·3 cm. 10⅝ × 8⅜ in. Fitzwilliam Museum, Cambridge

82. *Hamlet and Ophelia* 1858 Pen and ink, 30·5 × 26·7 cm. 12 × 10½ in. British Museum, London

83. *The First Madness of Ophelia* 1864 Watercolour, 39·4 × 29·2 cm. 15½ × 11½ in. Art Gallery and Museum, Oldham

84. *Hamlet and Ophelia* 1866 Watercolour, 38·1 × 27·9 cm. 15 × 11 in. Private Collection

85. *Fanny Cornforth* 1865 Pencil, 24·8 × 34·9 cm. 9¾ × 13¾ in. Private Collection

86. *Woman Combing her Hair* 1864 Watercolour 36·2 × 33 cm. 14¼ × 13 in. Private Collection

87. *Morning Music* 1864 Watercolour, 30·5 × 27·3 cm. 12 × 10¾ in. Fitzwilliam Museum, Cambridge

88. *Woman with a Fan* 1870 Crayons, 95·9 × 71·1 cm. 37¾ × 28 in. City Museum and Art Gallery, Birmingham

89. *Death of a Wombat* 1869 Pen and ink, 17·8 × 11·4 cm. 7 × 4½ in. British Museum, London

90. H. Treffry Dunn *Rossetti's Sitting Room at 16, Cheyne Walk* 1872 Watercolour, 54 × 82·6 cm. 21¼ × 32½ in. National Portrait Gallery, London

91. *Fair Rosamund* 1861 52·1 × 41·9 cm. 20½ × 16½ in. National Museum of Wales, Cardiff

92. *A Fight for a Woman* 1865 Watercolour, 34·3 × 27·9 cm. 13½ × 11 in. The Detroit Institute of Arts, Michigan

93. *The Blue Bower* 1865 190·2 × 69·2 cm. 35½ × 27¼ in. Barber Institute of Fine Arts, University of Birmingham

94. *Astarte Syriaca* 1877 182·8 × 106·7 cm. 72 × 42 in. City Art Gallery, Manchester

95. *The Blessed Damozel* 1875-9 149·9 × 80 cm. 59 × 31½ in. Lady Lever Art Gallery, Port Sunlight

96. *Jane Morris in Icelandic Costume* c.1873 Pen and ink, 26·2 × 28·6 cm.

$14\frac{1}{4} \times 11\frac{1}{4}$ in. Private Collection

97. *Jane Morris* c.1873 Pencil, 29·8 × 26·4 cm. $11\frac{3}{4} \times 10\frac{3}{8}$ in. Fitzwilliam Museum, Cambridge

98. *Jane Morris* 1873 Pen and ink and wash, 22·5 × 17·8 cm. $8\frac{7}{8} \times 7$ in. Private Collection

99. *Desdemona's Death Song* c.1878-81 Pencil, 104·1 × 74·9 cm. 41 × $29\frac{1}{2}$ in. Private Collection

100. Study for *The Day Dream* 1878 Pastel and chalk, 104·8 × 76·8 cm. $41\frac{1}{4} \times 30\frac{1}{4}$ in. Ashmolean Museum, Oxford

I

The development of the art of Dante Gabriel Rossetti from the 1840s to his death in 1882 provides a fine example of the way in which the role of the artist in England changed in the course of the nineteenth century. The transition is from a directly critical, questioning and socially concerned response, to an escapist and complacent endorsement of the realities of life. In the literature of the same period the change can be plotted in the development from the biting and urgent social criticism of the early novels of Elizabeth Gaskell, Charles Kingsley and even Benjamin Disraeli,[1] to the relatively feeble, mannered and undemanding later work of the same authors.[2] On a more subtle level it can be perceived in the abandonment of the essentially 'social' concerns of the novelists of the 1840s by their successors; thus Thackeray, Trollope and George Eliot wrote essentially moral, intellectual or psychological—above all 'individual'— novels in which personal crises rather than social conflicts are the central features of the plots.[3] So with Rossetti, there is a gradual change from the revolutionary originality and impact of paintings like *The Girlhood of Mary Virgin* (1849) (Colour Plate 1) and *Found* (begun 1854) (Colour Plate 8) to the febrile indulgence and empty formalism of *Astarte Syriaca* (1877) (Plate 94).

The transition is not an altogether neat one. There are artistic and literary exceptions, but the general direction of the movement is not in doubt. Essentially it is from the rejection of and opposition to the social realities of the early nineteenth century by Blake, Wordsworth, Shelley and others to the indifferent acquiescence in them that is represented by the late Victorian 'aesthetic' justification of 'art for art's sake'—the rationalization of the irrelevance of art. The transition is from the negation of society to its affirmation.

For Wordsworth art was an agency of man's struggle with nature and with his fellows. He was committed to the realization of a new society:

> Not in Utopia—subterranean fields—
> Or some secreted island, Heaven knows where!
> But in the very world, which is the world
> Of all of us—the place where, in the end
> We find our happiness, or not at all![4]

By the 1890s the hero of a notorious play, *Axel*, described by W. B. Yeats as 'the new sacred book of the arts' would remark when on the verge of an 'aesthetic' suicide and remonstrated with by his lover—'As for living, our servants will do that for us.'[5]

In the intervening years the divorce of 'art' from social life became almost total, and though it is not my purpose to examine the reasons or consequences of this in any great depth it is essential to an understanding of Rossetti's art to appreciate his place in this historical and cultural process. There can be no doubt that the underlying reasons for the altered social position and social concerns of the artist are to be found in the changing relations of production and ownership, as a result of the rapid development of industrial capitalism in Britain after 1790.[6] It would be superficial and reductive to apply uncritically Marx's famous formulation of the relationship of aesthetic forms to economic ones, of ideological 'superstructure' to economic 'base',[7] but it is central to recognize its importance to any consideration of artistic endeavour and especially so in a period of such rapid flux as the middle years of the nineteenth century.

18

1 *Gabriele Rossetti* 1853

2 *Self Portrait* 1847

Dante Gabriel Rossetti, born in 1828, was a precocious child and learnt both to draw and to read at an early age. When he was four he was content with drawings of his rocking horse,[8] but by the age of six he was familiar with all the works of Shakespeare, Scott and Dante his namesake, and was drawing illustrations for these and other romantic tales in a conventional but highly competent fashion. He entered the school of Kings College, London, at the age of nine, and there he learnt Latin, Greek, French and German to add to the Italian that he already knew. At the time his father, Gabriele (Plate 1), was the Professor of Italian at the College. He had been curator of sculpture at the Naples Museum and one of Rossini's librettists, but since 1821 had been a political refugee, having been forced to flee the tyranny of King Ferdinand because of his publicly expressed democratic and nationalist sentiments. In London he had prospered and married Frances Polidori who was herself half Italian. They lived in Charlotte Street, and until Gabriele died in 1854 the atmosphere of the house remained Italian and radical. The failure of the European revolutionary upheavals in 1830 and again in 1848 meant that many intellectual dissidents had to leave their native lands, and London became a home for many of them. Among the Italians Mazzini and the poet Foscolo are perhaps the best known, but there were many others, and a number of these revolutionaries and exiles made the Rossetti household the centre of their social and intellectual life. There can be little doubt that this atmosphere of romantic intrigue and intellectual democratic theorizing deeply affected the life, the style and the outlook of the Rossetti sons. Indeed William, Gabriel's younger brother, who became a most able and energetic art critic, editor and propagandist, was in the 1880s to become an active militant on the fringes of the reviving anarchist and socialist movements.[9]

When, therefore, in 1846, at eighteen, Gabriel entered the Schools of the Royal Academy to study art (having already spent four years in a private drawing school) he was already a worldly, rebellious and imaginative young man. A fellow student's description gives a graphic endorsement of what might otherwise have seemed a somewhat flatteringly romantic self-portrait (Plate 2). 'Thick, beautiful, and closely-curled masses of rich, brown and neglected hair fell about an ample brow, and almost to the wearer's shoulders; strong eyebrows marked with their dark shadows a pair of rather sunken eyes, in which a sort of fire, instinct with what may be called proud cynicism, burned with a furtive sort of energy. His rather high cheekbones were the more observable because his cheeks were roseless and hollow enough to indicate the waste of life and midnight oil to which the youth was addicted. Close shaving left bare his very full, not to say sensuous lips and square-cut masculine chin. Rather below the middle height and with a slightly rolling gait, Rossetti came forward among his fellows with a jerking step, tossed the falling hair back from his face, and, having both hands in his pockets, faced the student world with an *insouciant* air which savoured of thorough self-reliance. A bare throat, a falling ill kept collar, boots not over familiar with brushes, black and well worn habiliments including not the ordinary jacket of the period but a loose dress-coat which had once been new—these were the outward and visible signs of a mood which cared even less for appearances than the art student of those days was accustomed to care, which undoubtedly was little enough!'[10]

But he was not only a casual and self-confident art student. He was a poet, and a poet whose achievement was already considerable. By 1848, when he was twenty, he had written many of his best poems including 'The Blessed Damozel' and 'My Sister's Sleep', and he had made meticulous verse translations of early Italian poetry, including Dante's *Vita Nuova* (not published till 1861). He continued to write and translate prolifically through the 1850s, and again after a pause following his wife's death in 1862. Rossetti's poems bear a very close relation indeed to his painting—he wrote pictorially, and he painted poetically, but he also regularly wrote poems specifically to accompany pictures and had them engraved on the frames or even occasionally inscribed them on the canvas. Likewise he painted scenes that he had previously treated as poems.[11]

It is this intricate link between the poems and the paintings that draws Rossetti into the mainstream of nineteenth-century romantic literary culture: the more so as he played a crucial role in reviving interest in, and appreciation of, the work of Blake and Keats, two romantics who played key roles in the development of Romanticism and its transformation from social critique to escapist indulgence. In 1847 Rossetti bought from William Palmer (Samuel Palmer's brother) for ten shillings a notebook that had belonged to William Blake and which he had used from 1787 to 1818. Rossetti kept and studied it all his life. Filled with drafts of poems, with portraits, sketches, epigrams and essays on the state of art and the position of the artist in English society, it was clearly a document which Blake himself valued very highly.[12] Included among the verse are drafts of some of Blake's most savage attacks on the exploitation of developing English capitalism such as 'The Chimney Sweep' and 'Holy Thursday':

Is this a holy thing to see
In a rich and fruitful land
Babes reduced to misery
Fed with cold and usurous hand

Is that trembling cry a song
Can it be a song of joy
And so great a number poor
'Tis a land of poverty

And their sun does never shine
And their fields are bleak and bare
And their ways are filled with thorns
'Tis eternal winter there

But perhaps the passages that the young Rossetti would have felt most directly applied to him as an aspiring artist were the blunt comments which Blake had to make on Joshua Reynolds whose *Discourses on Art* were in Blake's time, and still in Rossetti's, the most influential and inescapable statement of the nature of art and the artist's education. 'Can I speak with too great contempt', Blake wrote, 'of such contemptible fellows.' And he went on to attack the influence of Reynolds among both artists and connoisseurs. The works of those whom Reynolds admired and which contemporary English painters strove to emulate—Rubens, Rembrandt and Correggio—were brusquely dismissed as 'labours of imbecility', 'weak and vulgar . . . daubs', while English art critics were ridiculed: 'Most Englishmen when they look at a picture immediately set about looking for points of light and clap the picture in a dark corner . . . This is like looking for epigrams in Homer.'

This assault on the values and aspirations of contemporary English art struck a sympathetic chord in Rossetti who found himself profoundly out of sympathy with the murky tones and contrived highlights of the imitation old masters which Reynolds' advocacy of the 'grand style' had popularized.

A more problematic comment of Blake's and one which perhaps also struck a chord in Rossetti, provides a possible clue to his subsequent abandonment of the principle of 'Truth to nature' which was to become one of the fundamental slogans of the Pre-Raphaelite Brotherhood. 'No man of sense', wrote Blake, 'ever supposes that copying from Nature is the Art of Painting—if the Art is no more than this it is no better than any other manual labour—anybody may do it and the fool often will.' The difference between Rossetti's art and that of his most important fellow Pre-Raphaelite, William Holman Hunt, is to be found here. Rossetti's artistic creed was to become one not of fidelity to external nature but to his own inner experience. It was ultimately to reject reality and sublimate it by giving priority to his own fantasies and self-expression.[13] And for all his concern with reality, Blake provided in his notebook a rationale for this artistic divorce from the real world.

Rossetti had bought the Blake notebook in April 1847. Eleven months later, in March 1848, he had left the Academy Schools and was receiving private tuition from Ford Madox Brown, a moderately successful painter of historical genre scenes, who had been trained in Belgium, France and Italy (Plate 3). For some years Rossetti had noticed and admired his work in the annual exhibitions, but when he saw his painting of *Wycliffe Reading his Translation of the Bible to John of Gaunt* (Plate 4) at the 'Free Exhibition' at Hyde Park Corner he resolved to meet and work with Brown, seeing the tutor-pupil relationship as a possible means of escape from the academic drudgery of the Academy Schools. Brown later told the story of how, on receiving Rossetti's florid letter of praise and request for tuition ('the other glorious works you have exhibited have successively ruined my admiration, and kept me standing on the same spot for fabulous lengths of time')[14], he had assumed that he was being made fun of and went round to visit Rossetti with a stout stick, ready to use it if need be.[15] But finding him to be in earnest he accepted him as a student without charge.

The picture of Brown's which had so excited Rossetti was indeed an original and unusual piece of work, quite different both from his own earlier work, and also from the common run of contemporary art. Begun in 1847 after his return from Rome, it is based on the techniques of the Nazarenes, a group of German painters who had formed a semi-religious fraternity in Rome where they hoped to regenerate art through the imitation of the early Italian masters. Clarity of colour and outline, simplicity of composition and directness of observation and of appeal are characteristics of the painting of the Nazarenes which Brown reproduces, and the awkwardness of posture, brilliance of colour, and angularity of detailing which result are all features that were to become prominent in Pre-Raphaelite art. Technically indeed he anticipated one of the procedures which the Pre-Raphaelites used. He painted the whole picture on an undercoat of white: 'nothing like a good coating of white to get a good sunny colour,' he noted in his diary.[16]

In its choice of subject, too, Brown's painting has complex and evocative connotations. The winter of 1847-8 saw the culmination of the great progressive democratic struggle which had been a dominant feature of the social and political development of almost all the countries in Europe for the past twenty years. In 1848 one after another of these movements, mainly bourgeois and anti-feudal in tone, were defeated at the hands of the ruling class. In this context, this conjunction of economic and political struggle, a painting of Wycliffe is not as innocent as it might seem. Of course Brown was no secret revolutionary, and no more was Rossetti for all his connections with the *carbonari* and their secret societies, but Wycliffe had been a very open and persuasive revolutionary whose failure to achieve martyrdom is still cause for surprise. His doctrine was one of primitive communism, involving the confiscation of the wealth of the monasteries and the holding of all property in common by the righteous. His translation of the bible into English was of course deeply subversive of the mystification of the Catholic church, and Brown's painting therefore, read in the necessary historical context (as Rossetti may well have done) is by no means a neutral or unengaged work.

But working with Brown was less than a total success, as the elder artist's ideas of the proper means of learning to paint were not so very different from those of the Academy Schools. He first set Rossetti to copy a little painting of his own of two angels watching over the crown of thorns (Plate 5) and then to paint a still life of a group of bottles and artistic bric-à-brac that was lying around in his studio (Plate 6).[17] Rossetti finished the first in a sketchy sort of way, but before the second was complete he was already looking for an excuse to stop.

It came in May when he saw at the Academy exhibition *The Eve of St Agnes* (Plate 7) by one of his fellow pupils at the Schools, William Holman Hunt. He knew Hunt slightly, but now approached him with an enthusiasm comparable to that with which he had surprised and alarmed the modest Madox Brown. 'Rossetti came up to me', recalled Hunt, 'repeating with emphasis his praise, and loudly declaring that my picture . . . was the best in the collection.'[18] Within weeks Rossetti had begun to share a studio with Hunt, and having abandoned the still life of 'the pickle jars' was embarked with Hunt's encouragement on an altogether more ambitious painting which was based on a drawing that he had previously done for the Cyclographic Club—a club of fellow students who circulated graphic designs among themselves on a regular basis. This picture was to be *The Girlhood of Mary Virgin* (Colour Plate 1) which will be discussed in

24

3 *Ford Madox Brown* 1852

4 Ford Madox Brown *John Wycliffe Reading his*
Translation of the Bible to John of Gaunt in the Presence
of Chaucer and Gower 1848

5 *Angels Watching over the Crown of Thorns* 1848

6 *Bottles* 1848

7 William Holman Hunt *The Eve of St Agnes* 1848

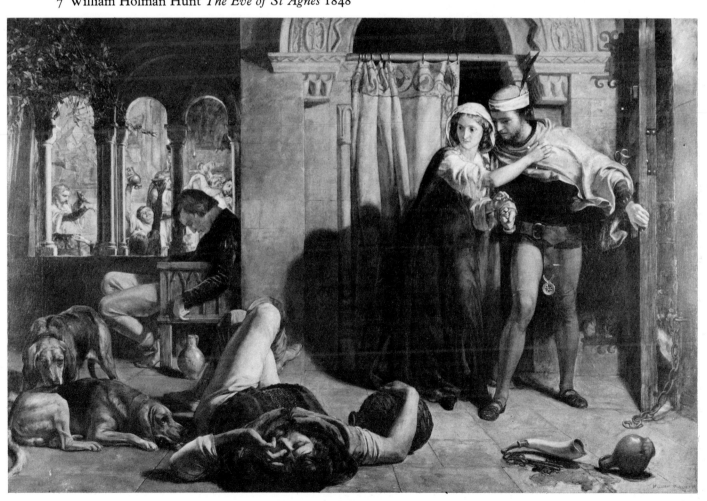

8 *Faust—Gretchen and Mephistopheles in the Church* 1848

9 *Faust—Gretchen and Mephistopheles in the Church* 1848

the next chapter. Unfortunately the drawing on which it was based is lost but we do have a number of Rossetti's drawings of the period which give an idea of what it must have been like, and which enable us to plot some of the stylistic changes which his art was undergoing in these months just before the foundation of the Pre-Raphaelite Brotherhood.

Goethe's *Faust* was a favourite book of Rossetti's and there are several surviving examples of illustrations from it done in 1848. Plates 8 and 9 show two versions of the same moment: Gretchen (Margaret) in church before her seduction by Faust, with Mephistopheles whispering in her ear. The characters, the furnishings and the settings are virtually identical, but the spirit and style of the drawings could scarcely be less similar. The first is a relatively open and florid exercise that looks backward to recent trends in book illustration by Gilbert and others and relates to the work of countless undistinguished artists of the 1840s and earlier. In the second, which can only be later by a matter of weeks, we are at once in the claustrophobic, fearful and private world that Rossetti was to explore and elaborate for the rest of his life. No longer are we distanced from the drawing by the conventional technique and the motif of Faust and Mephistopheles (in another incarnation) watching the action from the corners of the drawing—conventionalized horror has been replaced by something much less tangible and obvious, but much more impressively oppressive—the latter effect achieved by the heavy hatching, the graphic detail and the spiky forms.

This second version of Faust was almost certainly one of the three drawings submitted to the Cyclographic Club. It was considered but discarded by Rossetti as the basis of the picture he was to paint in Hunt's studio.[19] The third was a drawing of *Genevieve* from Coleridge's poem 'Love' which shows the nervously linear and spiky style further developed (Plate 10). Drawn one night and not finished till six in the morning, it also provides one of the first examples of Rossetti's conscious and deliberate medievalizing escapism, a tendency which was soon to dominate his work:

> She leaned against the armed man,
> The statue of the armed knight,
> She stood and listened to my lay,
> Amid the lingering light.

Although there are examples of a more robust or at least less consciously anachronistic romanticism in drawings from Edgar Allan

10 *Genevieve* 1848

11 *Ululame c.* 1848

12 *The Sleeper c.* 1847

13 *The Raven c.* 1847

Poe (Plates 11-13) which also illuminate the rapid development of his draughtsmanship in the summer months of 1848, it is the deliberate medievalizing of *Genevieve* that perhaps throws most light on his admiration for Hunt's *Eve of St Agnes*, and in turn illustrates the way in which his art advanced latent tendencies in the aesthetic of English Romanticism.

Hunt's painting was of course derived from Keats' medievalizing poem of the same name, but it is not now readily appreciated that Keats was in 1848 a relatively forgotten and unread poet. None of his poems had been republished since his death in 1821 and none of them had ever before formed the subject of a painting at the Academy. Hunt recalled how he had bought his copy of the poems from a bookstall in the bin labelled 'this lot 4d.'. In spite of this relative obscurity Keats' work was admired too by Rossetti, and this common love provided the foundation of the otherwise somewhat improbable friendship that developed between the two.

Indeed, the Pre-Raphaelite Brotherhood was to be deeply and constantly indebted to Keats and his ideas expressed through his poems and letters (first published by Monckton Milnes in 1848 and avidly read by Rossetti and Hunt as soon as they became available). But though this influence provided the stimulus for the production of some remarkable and original paintings, it also provided the aesthetic justification for the transformation of art from a position of engagement to one of social indifference. For Keats had argued the divorce of art from life—an argument of great and increasing attraction to the mid-century artists and poets, but to none more so than to Rossetti who was soon to develop and clarify it greatly. Keats saw art as a *compensation* for the poverty and inadequacy of actual life, not as an agency to overcome it. Beauty for him was no longer real (as it had been for Wordsworth) but had its source in a separate world, in the imagination or subjectivity of the artist. The perfect illusion was to be preferred to imperfect reality, and from this it was only a short step, and a step which Rossetti found only too attractive, to the conscious renunciation of life in favour of art.[20] This step was never taken by Hunt, who was consequently to become the focus of derisive criticism by a later generation. The Pre-Raphaelite Brotherhood in its initial conception represented a conscious attempt to relate art directly to life and was therefore an objectively progressive force. However, the causes of its decay and the consequent divorce of its components were present, and indeed prominent, at its inception. Within a few years Rossetti and Millais had succumbed to these contradictions, leaving only Hunt as a querulous and idiosyncratic defender of the original ideal.

2

It is not too much of an oversimplification to distinguish two contrasting and competing strands in the history of the art of the era of developing English capitalism. Each strand can be broadly defined by its response to industrialization and the corresponding social and economic changes.

Alongside the perennial run of portraits and landscapes which changed little from generation to generation (though they too responded in subtle ways) can be seen what might be crudely but conveniently labelled 'conservative' and 'progressive' tendencies. Perhaps the three best-known (and best) representatives of the conservative tendency were Sir David Wilkie, Sir Edwin Landseer and William Etty. Technically they all aspired to paint imitation old masters in the style sanctified by Sir Joshua Reynolds and characterized by the use of sombre colours, murky tones, brilliant highlights, formal compositions, and, often, traditional Renaissance subjects such as, for example, *The Judgement of Paris* (Plate 14).

14 William Etty *The Judgement of Paris* 1826

15 Sir David Wilkie *The Irish Whiskey Still* 1840

But their conservatism was much more subtle than this brief characterization of their art might imply, and it by no means represented a blind ignorance of, or hostility to, social change. Etty for instance specialized in a form of pictorial pornography that was becoming socially acceptable in the earlier decades of the century. He was the first English painter to specialize in the female nude, and though there can be no doubt either of his technical competence or of his own personal obsession with the subject, the fact is that he was plentifully and lucratively supplying a demand for sexist images redolent of human exploitation.[1]

Etty was not quite respectable enough to achieve knighthood, unlike Landseer and Wilkie, both of whom became highly regarded figures in aristocratic and court circles. Technically their work in most respects resembled that of Etty, and today its bituminous and heavily varnished nature renders it generally even more murky and gloomy than when first painted. But the choice of subject matter is generally a sentimental and implausible genre—selected one might guess primarily to bolster the prejudices and improbable fantasies of their patrons, fantasies which of course the artists broadly speaking shared. Thus sheep dogs mourn at the gravesides of their shepherds, guerrillas return wounded and defeated from battle against 'legitimate' authority, and, in a peculiarly revealing and evocative example (Plate 15), the Irish are portrayed as a starving and impoverished lot, but with only themselves to blame because of their idle and drunken habits. As ideological statements this and other of Wilkie's Irish subjects painted in the late 1830s and 1840s are directly evocative of the 'civilizing mission' of the British Imperialists. The very high proportion of the pictures which ended up in noble or even royal collections makes an interesting contrast to the fate of the work of more progressive contemporaries, and in the 1850s to that of the Pre-Raphaelites.

Side by side with these established and successful purveyors of wish fulfilment to an historically doomed aristocracy, there were artists who were trying in various ways to adapt their approach to the revolutionary economic and social developments of the time. As long ago as the 1770s painters like Joseph Wright of Derby had begun to come to terms with the visual consequences of developing industry, and some of Turner's most eloquent canvases are on this general theme (e.g. *Rain, Steam and Speed*), but by the second quarter of the nineteenth century efforts were being made to confront and illustrate the social as well as the material reality. Alfred Elmore's ambitious if awkward attempts to paint allegories of *The Origin of the Stocking*

16 Alfred Elmore *The Origin of the Stocking Frame* 1847

17 Richard Redgrave *The Poor Teacher* 1844

Frame (Plate 16) and *The Invention of the Combing Loom* (Nottingham Art Gallery) are interesting early works by an artist who in later life was to deal seriously and strikingly with other themes from contemporary life.[2] Perhaps more interesting, because a substantial success, was Richard Redgrave's *Poor Teacher* (Plate 17) of 1844. A picture dealing with the social *déclassement* of the younger daughters of the lesser bourgeoisie, the subject has clear affinities with Dickens and other social novelists.[3] The fact that Redgrave painted four replicas, so great was the demand, and that the version reproduced (now in the Victoria and Albert Museum) was bought by John Sheepshanks, a cloth manufacturer from Leeds and thus the epitome of the successful entrepreneurial bourgeois, gives it a special interest. In the years following, pictures that dealt with modern social and economic problems in a relatively straightforward and sympathetic way were not uncommon at the Academy, and one of these, Mulready's *'Train up a Child the way he should go'*, provides direct links between the new patronage, the new type of subject and the technical innovation that was simultaneously developing. Though Mulready considered it one of his finest achievements the picture seems strangely forced and improbable to us today—a befrocked and obviously terrified child is being egged on by two exquisite ladies to give alms to a couple of murderous beggars. In 1841 though, when it was painted, this direct confrontation with social reality represented a noteworthy breath of fresh air in an otherwise claustrophobic artistic hot house. It was bought (ironically but significantly) by Thomas Baring, the financier and banker. On the whole, Mulready's subject matter was less directly contemporary in reference, but much of it was timeless rather than deliberately anachronistic. *The Sonnet* (Plate 18) of 1839, and also bought by Sheepshanks of Leeds, provides an example of technical originality that was to be taken up and exploited by the Pre-Raphaelites ten years later. The bright colours and careful detail are indeed reminiscent of Pre-Raphaelite paintings, and not surprisingly, since the whole was painted over a white ground with the translucent colours laid on thinly afterwards.[4] But Mulready was not alone in developing and extending the limits of artistic technique. Since the time of Blake (who had admired excessively the Gothic and the art of Raphael, Giotto and other early Italians) there had been a tendency in many quarters to look to pre-Renaissance art to provide the stimulus for new departures and new ideas, and one of the most fruitful consequences was a new affection for pure colours and linear form.

18 William Mulready *The Sonnet* 1839

This historicism was a highly complex aesthetic response common to nearly every country in Europe in the early years of the century. Undoubtedly triggered by industrial development, it affected all the arts to a greater or lesser degree and Keats' medievalizing that we have already considered was one aspect of it. Another was Pugin's powerful defence and advocacy of the Gothic. In terms of aesthetic theory it took the form of numerous studies of the art of the pre-Renaissance period, and the conscious imitation of pre-Renaissance styles and techniques by numerous artists.

As Britain was the most highly developed capitalist country in terms of industrial output one would expect this response to be most marked there, and indeed it was, but it was not confined to Britain. In Italy, as we have already seen, a group of German painters, the Nazarenes, had formed a semi-religious fraternity in 1810 whose aim was to regenerate art by imitation of the early masters. In France, even earlier, in 1800 a group of pupils of David[5] including J.A.D. Ingres had styled themselves *les Primitifs*, whilst one of their number, Maurice Quay, had even called himself *Pré-Raphaelite*. None of Quay's works of the period survive, but there are clear reminiscences of early art in the work of Ingres who had said of the Orcagna frescoes in the Campo Santo in Pisa which dated from *c.* 1350, 'It is on one's knees that one should study these men.' Reproductions of the same frescoes were to be studied by Rossetti, Millais and Hunt on the evening that they decided to form the Pre-Raphaelite Brotherhood.

France also saw the first publication of Rio's *Poésie de l'art Chrétien* (1836) which was soon translated into English and became highly influential. It is interesting that the translator, Ambrose Phillips de l'Isle, was a close friend of Pugin's and a militant Catholic proselytizer, thus providing a direct link—one of several—between the gothic revival, Roman Catholicism and 'pre-raphaelitism'. But most of the important books on early art were written in England, among them Lindsay's *Sketches of the History of Christian Art* (1847) and Mrs Jamesone's *Poetry of Sacred and Legendary Art* (1848). 'Only by studying the primitives', wrote Lindsay, 'their purity, innocent naïveté, childlike grace and simplicity, their freshness, fearlessness and utter freedom from affectation, their yearning after all things truthful, lovely and of good report can art become great again.' These books, however, were published in an intellectual atmosphere which had been prepared for them by a number of other influences and events.

Most clearly indicative, perhaps, of the changing climate of opinion about the arts in Britain was the decision in 1843 (following a Royal Commission) to decorate the newly built Houses of Parliament with frescoes in the ancient manner. Not only did this officially promote an interest in fourteenth- and fifteenth-century art, but it also associated the recently reformed and increasingly bourgeois House of Commons directly with the progressive tendency that this art represented. It is by no means irrelevant that the same House of Commons which declared that public money spent on such art was 'directly instrumental in creating new objects of industry and of enjoyment and therefore in adding, at the same time, to the wealth of the country',[6] was two years later to establish finally and irreversibly the authority of industrial property over landed property by repealing the Corn Laws.[7]

In fact the frescoes proved something of a disappointment, and the scheme was not completed till the 1860s, but the first one to be finished was by William Dyce, a Scotsman who had been friendly with the Nazarenes in Rome and whose art was already in the 1840s displaying an explicitly 'primitive' and 'early Italian' character (Plate 19). His illustration of Coleridge's *Christabel* (Plate 20) provides an interesting link between the medievalizing of the poem and the early Italian manner, recalling as it does Kingsley's comment (when reviewing Mrs Jamesone) that the young most admired 'the sweetness, the purity, the rapt devotion and the saintly virtue which shines forth from the painting of Fra Angelico'. (Though in fact the model here was the then much less well-known Botticelli.)

Like Mulready, Dyce was not only experimenting with new techniques in the decades before 1850, but he was also to become an admirer and in some respects adherent of the Pre-Raphaelite Brotherhood after its formation. It was indeed he who first made Ruskin examine the work of the Brotherhood with care though he can hardly have anticipated the momentous consequences of Ruskin's conversion to the Pre-Raphaelite cause. Indeed Ruskin was later to criticize Dyce for deriving his inspiration from the imitation of early art rather than the direct observation of nature, and one has to acknowledge that Ruskin was broadly right. Similarly Ruskin was to define Mulready's shortcomings by the same materialist yardstick, 'I hardly know how to speak of Mulready; in delicacy and completion of drawing, and splendour of colour he takes his place beside . . . the Pre-Raphaelites, but he has throughout his career displayed no definiteness in choice of subject. He must be named among the painters who have studied with industry and made themselves great by doing so; but, having obtained a consummate method of execution, he has thrown it away on subjects altogether uninteresting, or above his power, or unfit for pictorial representation . . . Mulready, therefore, while he has always produced exquisite pieces of painting has failed in doing anything that can be of true or extensive use.'[8]

41

19 William Dyce *Virgin and Child* 1838

20 William Dyce *Christabel* 1855

With Ruskin's analysis of the essential failure of both Dyce and Mulready we return to Rossetti and Hunt. For in the work of Ruskin, Hunt, Rossetti and Millais found the intellectual stimulus that they needed to unite effectively the two existing strands of the progressive movement in English art. And to the developments in technique and in subject matter they added, thanks to Ruskin, a third, a materialistic view of the world which was expressed as an attempt to paint reality directly and as it was with no intervening conventions or mannerisms.

One or two artists had already begun to paint meticulously 'photographic' representations of reality in the 1840s, most notably William 'Bird's Nest' Hunt, so called because of his favourite subject matter, and J. F. Lewis whose precise and conscientious paintings of (mainly) exotic eastern scenes were greatly admired by Ruskin and praised towards the end of *Modern Painters*, 'I have never seen more than four works of John Lewis on the walls of the water colour exhibition; I have counted forty from other hands; but have found in the end that the forty were a multiplication of one, and the four a concentration of one.' The first volume of *Modern Painters* had been published in 1844, and in 1847 Holman Hunt had stayed up all night to read a borrowed copy. It is a long, complex and confusing book but it is full of perceptions, assertions and arguments about art that echoed and crystallized Hunt's, and through him Rossetti's, artistic concerns and aspirations. Denouncing art in Rome where 'among all students, the authority of their predecessors in art is supreme and without appeal, and the mindless copyist studies Rafaelle, but not what Rafaelle studied,' Ruskin goes on to praise Orcagna, Fra Angelico, Giotto and Cimabue whose 'burning messages' are insufficiently appreciated in comparison to the 'tricks of chiaroscuro' of later artists, because in spite of their 'intrinsic excellence' it is always 'a labour rather than a pleasure to read them' for the vulgar and shallow contemporary critic. These critics, and the artists they admire, 'pander more fatally every year to the vicious English taste which can enjoy nothing but what is theatrical' so that 'Brilliancy and rapidity of execution are everywhere sought as the highest good'.

Against this superficial, empty, and flashy art he set an art of ideas, for art, he argued, was a language which must be used to express ideas and not merely for its own sake: 'the critic must distinguish what is language and what is thought, and rank and praise pictures chiefly for the latter, considering the former as a totally inferior excellence.' From this it followed that 'the greatest picture is that which conveys to the spectator the greatest number of the greatest ideas,' and since the 'ideas of truth' are the greatest of all ideas, 'nothing can be beautiful which is not true'.

Ruskin is already entering deep philosophical water, but plunges on seizing only a distinction between 'material truth' (i.e. imitation) and 'moral truth' as an intellectual lifebelt. 'Truths', he says, 'are valuable in proportion as they are particular and valueless in proportion as they are general.' The real truthfulness therefore (and by extension beauty) of a painting is 'in proportion to the number and variety of the facts illustrated.' He goes on to urge the artist to 'concentrate the greatest quantity of thought on the least possible space of canvas', if necessary to take 'a twelvemonth's thought' over a picture, and to ask himself, 'can my details be added to? Is there a single space in the picture where I can crowd in another thought? Is there a curve in it which I can modulate, a line which I can vary, a vacancy I can fill? Is there a single spot which the eye, by any peering or prying, can fathom or exhaust? If so my picture is imperfect.'

This serious, puritanical and moral approach to art found a ready response in Hunt, and though there is little in Rossetti's later life or writings to indicate that he really understood the implications of this approach to painting or was prepared to carry through the principles with any determination, we must remember that he was now, in the summer of 1848, a drop-out from the Academy Schools and from Brown's tuition, yet desperately anxious to establish himself as an artist and a fervent admirer of Hunt in whose friendship and help lay the only acceptable resolution of his problems.

It is no wonder therefore that Rossetti accepted as his own Ruskin's doctrines which Hunt had already totally identified himself with. Hunt felt, he later said, as though *Modern Painters* had been written 'expressly for him'. And the painting that Rossetti worked on in Hunt's studio that summer—*The Girlhood of Mary Virgin* (Colour Plate 1)—was painted according to these principles, Rossetti having gone 'to nature in all singleness of heart [to] walk with her laboriously and trustingly, having no other thoughts than how best to penetrate her meaning and remember her instruction; rejecting nothing, selecting nothing and scorning nothing'. Apart from its visual fidelity both the subject and the symbolism display a 'solemnity and earnestness' of purpose that wholly satisfy Ruskin's criteria.

It is an ambitious and complex painting, the problems of which taxed Rossetti's abilities to the utmost, and indeed on occasion defeated them. Madox Brown, who took a continuing interest in his ex-pupil's work, and with whom Rossetti was to develop a close friendship, recounted in his diary a visit which ended with Rossetti 'lying, howling, on his belly' in exasperation, and another occasion on which problems with painting drapery reduced him to a state of incomprehensible profanity.[9]

Begun in July or August 1848 it was only just completed in time for the opening of the 'Free Exhibition'[10] on 24 March 1849, but both its planning and its execution were laborious and time-consuming operations. Numerous studies were made, while the landscape background was painted from nature in the late summer before any figures were drawn in. When they were added they were painted directly, not from professional models or lay figures, but from Rossetti's mother as St Anne, the Virgin's mother, his sister Christina as the Virgin, and a family servant as St Joachim, the Virgin's father, and all contemporary critics agree that they are good likenesses. Perhaps this is not surprising in view of the rate of progress ('St Anne put on a red hood today', he wrote to a friend in November) but such unidealized fidelity to the physiognomy of their models was characteristic of early Pre-Raphaelite painting. It had hitherto been seldom practised—certainly not as an article of faith. One of the most telling indices of Rossetti's alienation from the spirit of 1848 indeed is the increasing extent to which the features of his models become stylized and subordinated to the inner compulsions of his art.

While work proceeded Rossetti read more Keats, and completed his translation of Dante's *Vita Nuova*. Keats, he wrote to his brother William, 'seems to have been a glorious fellow, and says in one place (to my great delight) that having just looked over a folio of the first and second schools of Italian painting he has come to the conclusion that the early men surpassed even Raphael himself'.[11] The *Vita Nuova* he thought offered 'admirable opportunities for pictorial representation',[12] and it is interesting to observe that as early as November 1848 he listed in a letter some of the major themes that he proposed to paint, some of which, like *Dante's Dream*, were to preoccupy him virtually until his death, and one of which, *Dante Interrupted while Drawing an Angel on the Anniversary of Beatrice's Death*, he had already drawn (Plate 21). This drawing, dated September 1848, is the earliest of all his drawings from Dante, and actually pre-dates by a few weeks the foundation of the Pre-Raphaelite Brotherhood from whose aesthetic confines Dante and other Italianate subjects were to provide an escape route. As with Keats, so another of the factors that was to disrupt the Brotherhood was present, not merely as an interest but as an object of aesthetic practice, before its inception. The drawing itself shows clear affinities to the earlier *Gretchen and Mephistopheles* and to *Genevieve* which had been drawn only a few weeks earlier. Now badly rubbed, its flat and two-dimensional linearity are still very evident, while its severe but idiosyncratic archaisms were all features to be developed in the course of the next few years.

21 *Dante Drawing an Angel on the First Anniversary of the
Death of Beatrice* 1848

22 *Dante Drawing an Angel on the First Anniversary of the
Death of Beatrice* 1849

One evening in (probably) October, Rossetti and Hunt, and Hunt's friend John Millais, a brilliant and impressionable art student at the Royal Academy Schools, while looking over and admiring some engravings of the fourteenth-century frescoes by Orcagna and others in the Campo Santo in Pisa (those which Ingres had so much admired) decided to give a more formal character to their rebellion against contemporary artistic practice, and, as much in jest as earnest, decided to call themselves 'The Pre-Raphaelite Brotherhood'. 'Pre-Raphaelite' because they decided with the impetuousness born of ignorance that everything fine in art pre-dated Raphael 'before the showy followers of Michelangelo had grafted their Dead Sea fruit on to the vital tree'. A 'brotherhood' at Rossetti's suggestion for reasons apparently theatrical and romantic—for 'brotherhood' was the term of self-identification commonly employed by groups of Italian revolutionaries or bandits (or both).

Each was already a member of any number of unofficial student societies—Rossetti's published letters of this period are full of references to incipient, existing or moribund artistic and literary groupings, so the initial formation of the Brotherhood cannot have any great significance attached to it. Events were to dignify it with greater importance than it really deserved, but there was, to begin with at least, a fair measure of agreement about just what the aims of the brethren were. 'The name of our Body,' wrote Hunt, 'was meant to keep in our minds our determination ever to do battle against the frivolous art of the day, which had for its ambition "Monkeyana ideas",[13] "Books of Beauty" and chorister boys whose forms were those of melted wax with drapery of no tangible texture.'[14]

Various others were enrolled as brethren. James Collinson, an able and interesting fellow-pupil whose few works display a more highly developed interest in the material reality of mid-Victorian Britain than almost any of his contemporaries, was the only other painter. Suffering from the endemic bourgeois disease of the time, a crisis of faith, which was aggravated by an unhappy love affair with Rossetti's religiose sister Christina, he resigned from the Brotherhood in 1850, renounced the world altogether and sought solace in a monastery. Thomas Woolner was also a fellow-pupil, but a sculptor, while F. G. Stephens and Gabriel's brother William were both to become professional art critics.

Meetings were held on a monthly basis, and obviously they were successful for the members took to addressing each other as brethren, and when, the following year, Rossetti reworked his drawing of *Dante Drawing an Angel on the Anniversary of Beatrice's Death*

Colour 1 *The Girlhood of Mary Virgin* 1849

(Plate 22) he gave it to Millais inscribing it 'Dante Gabriel Rossetti to his P R Brother John E Millais'. Similar signatures to letters and drawings became commonplace, and it was agreed by Rossetti, Millais, and Hunt that each should sign the picture that he was working on for the next spring with the monogram 'PRB'. Since the brethren were sworn to secrecy over the meaning of the initials this can only be seen as a little joke at the expense of the critics and the public—already perhaps the 'honesty' and 'seriousness of purpose' were becoming diluted.

The Girlhood of Mary Virgin was well received by the reviewers, and bought by the Marchioness of Bath for £80—a purchase probably not unconnected with the fact that Rossetti's aunt had been her governess and was to become a 'companion' to the family. Nor was the price paid at all bad. In February 1848, Etty, then at the height of his fame, sold a religious painting of a similar size to his extremely wealthy and established patron Gillott for £200,[15] while Madox Brown, Rossetti's teacher, was paid only £60 *p.a.* in 1853 as head-master of the North London Drawing School in Hampstead,[16] and was unable to sell the painting of *Wycliffe*, which Rossetti had so much admired in 1848, until 1852, and then only for £63. An alleged shortage of money became a constant refrain throughout Rossetti's life, and he, though generous with money when he had it, encouraged the illusion.[17] It is important to bear in mind that any such shortage had far more to do with his own personal extravagance and high standard of living than to his inability to command high prices for his work. As we shall see the financial pressures resulting from his expensive tastes had a very direct effect on his art.

The Girlhood is richly symbolic of virtue and of the life of Christ which it of course foreshadows. The young Mary embroiders on to a scarlet cloth an angel-held lily (symbol of purity) which rests on a pile of books whose spines are inscribed with various of the virtues—Fortitude, Temperance, Prudence, Faith, Hope and Charity. Meanwhile in the visual centre of the picture is a cross which serves for the time being as a trellis for ivy—a symbol of 'clinging memory'[18]—but inevitably, with the palm branch and thorn in the foreground and the crimson cloak beside it, prefigures the passion and crucifixion. Other references abound which together with the soft-hued palette and the flat laborious technique set the work apart from other contemporary religious paintings. It would be claiming too much to say that it really reflected fifteenth-century Italian practice, but in spite of the particularity of the models and the anachronistic books, the painting is something more than the conventional costume drama which passed for historical or religious art. Considering that Rossetti had never been out of England, and considering how few early Italian pictures he could have seen in London, in spite of the National Gallery's enlightened purchasing policy, *The Girlhood of Mary Virgin* does represent a remarkable attempt to fuse physical reality with anachronistic but symbolically and actually progressive technique and subject matter. For a virtually self-trained student of twenty it is an astonishing *tour de force*.

Encouraged by the success of his first offering Rossetti determined 'that I should come before the public next year as prominently as possible so as to succeed in establishing at once some degree of reputation'.[19] And to this end he set to work on his next picture, *Ecce Ancilla Domini!* (later retitled *The Annunciation* to evade accusations of Popery) (Colour Plate 2). Rossetti once again used his sister Christina as the model for the Virgin. The embroidered lily from the previous picture is now complete and hanging over the same peculiar collapsible embroidery table. But technically the resemblance to fifteenth-century painting is much closer. Partly this is because of the simplicity of the subject and the absence of clutter and stage props which so often betray the nineteenth-century origins of contemporary historicism. Partly it is because the subject (unlike that of his previous painting) was a traditional one among early artists. And partly it is because of the even paler tonality of the whole with the prevailing white only relieved by small clear patches of blue, red and yellow. It is certainly relevant to its appearance that in September and October 1849 while it was being conceived, Rossetti accompanied by Hunt made a brief visit to Paris, Brussels, Ghent and Bruges where he saw and greatly admired among others many early Netherlandish paintings by Memling and Van Eyck—'miraculous . . . most stupendous'[20] he called them. For though there is a clear Italian reference in *The Annunciation* its enclosed composition with a glimpse of landscape beyond (a feature which is found in many early Pre-Raphaelite works), and its meticulous naturalism with each hair individually painted, are really far closer to the work of the fifteenth-century artists of northern Europe.

It is a brave painting, in its stark colouring and bleakly realistic treatment of a theme that, above all others demanded mystic sentimentality at a time when the teaching of the church was under increasingly hostile rationalist attack. Not surprisingly, its bluntness allied to its Latin title was assumed to carry Catholic or at least very High Church connotations. And when, inadvertently, the meaning of the initials PRB was revealed to a journalist, the response of the critics

Colour 2 *Ecce Ancilla Domini! (The Annunciation)* 1850

Colour 3 *Ruth and Boaz* 1855

was almost pavlovian. Faced with paintings by a so-called 'Brotherhood', three of which were explicitly religious and probably Catholic in context (*The Annunciation*, Millais' *Christ in the House of his Parents* (Tate Gallery) and Hunt's *Converted British Family Sheltering a Christian Priest from the Persecution of the Druids* (Ashmolean Museum, Oxford)) and one of which seemed unduly concerned with the lot of the working class (Collinson's *Answering the Emigrant's Letter* (City Art Gallery, Manchester)), the responsible bourgeois journalist had no doubt where his duty lay. The Catholic church appeared to pose a threat to the hegemony of the English middle class that was second only to that posed by the recently defeated and currently quiescent proletariat. The legal restrictions on Catholicism had only recently been repealed, while English history in the 1840s had been punctuated by scares of various kinds about the machinations of the great Catholic powers of Europe which it is not unfair to compare with the anti-Bolshevik hysteria of the 1920s and 1940s and 1950s. These culminated in the so called 'Papal Aggression' of 1850 when the Roman Catholic hierarchy of bishops was reconstituted with a flamboyant encyclical from Rome that induced the Prime Minister, Lord John Russell, to write an open letter to the Bishop of Durham characterising 'the late aggression of the Pope upon our protestantism as insolent and insidious . . . no foreign prince . . . will be at liberty to fasten his fetters upon a nation which has so long and so nobly vindicated its right to freedom.' The entire press was in a state of uproar, and the government introduced the Ecclesiastical Titles Bill to give it powers to restrict the Catholic clergy.[21]

Physical (and by implication social) candour while less of a threat was no less offensive: 'If Mr Hunt will not give us beauty, at least let him refrain from idealizing vulgarity', commented the *Athenaeum* primly.[22]

The paintings of the Brotherhood, therefore, were greeted with a quite unreasoning intensity of abuse—'revolting', 'uncouth', 'all the objectionable peculiarities of the infancy of art', 'unhealthy', 'retrograde', 'perverse' were some of the epithets applied by the intellectual monthlies and quarterlies.

As might be expected, the impact of this hostility on a group of young men still in their early twenties was devastating. Rossetti wrote a riposte to the *Athenaeum* which the editor (then as now the self-appointed guardian of the 'freedom of the press') refused to print. The Brotherhood survived, but only just; and already Rossetti, having again exhibited separately from the others and thus avoided the worst of the critical strictures (as last year he had by exhibiting first apparently jumped the gun), was beginning to become estranged from the others.

Neither Hunt nor Rossetti were able to sell their pictures from the exhibition, and there is some evidence to show that Millais, having already agreed a sale, was forced to cut his price in order to complete it. Mutual recriminations abounded. The self-confident and hard headed Millais commented that people would be better advised to buy his pictures now when he was working for fame rather than in a few years time when he would be married and working for a wife and children. The indigent and sensitive Hunt with his commissions repudiated and with no private means—not even sufficient to buy himself a new canvas—fell back on the support of Augustus Egg and William Dyce, who were among the few Academicians prepared to give the Brotherhood any support. Dyce found him work restoring pictures for Trinity House, while Egg commissioned his next painting.

1850 also saw the resignation of Collinson from the Brotherhood, and though in the same year the first works were painted in the manner of the PRB by artists who were not themselves members,[23] the final collapse could not long be postponed. In May 1851 William Michael Rossetti ceased to keep the 'Pre-Raphaelite Journal' in which he had recorded their meetings and doings. In 1852 Woolner emigrated to Australia, and when in 1854 Hunt went on the first of his lengthy trips to the Middle East only two months after Millais had been elected an Associate of the Royal Academy against which the revolt had in theory been directed, Rossetti wrote 'the whole round table is dissolved'.

Millais' worldly success, which was later to achieve stupendous proportions with his income exceeding £30,000 *p.a.* in the 1880s was still some years away however, and in the immediate aftermath of the 1850 *débâcle* he set to work with Hunt on another Pre-Raphaelite picture from nature. Hunt's steadfast adherence to his own conception of the Brotherhood's original principles, which was to lead him in due course to the Holy Land as the only appropriate place to paint pictures illustrative of the life of Christ, was insufficient to hold the independent-minded Rossetti in check, though the more conventional and less imaginative Millais was to remain to a considerable degree under his influence for at least another six years.

Hunt was however, able to persuade Rossetti to accompany him to Sevenoaks in Kent to paint from nature in Knole Park the background to his next picture. The resulting fiasco demonstrates quite clearly the way in which the artists were diverging, and the extent to which

Colour 4 *Girl Singing to a Lute* 1853

Rossetti was beginning to abandon the original principles of fidelity to reality and the inspiration of early Italian or Netherlandish art.

While Hunt worked on the background of *Valentine Rescuing Sylvia from Proteus* (Plate 23) Rossetti complained about the rain, and (more interestingly) about the subject matter. 'The cold here is awful when it does not rain,' he wrote to his friend Jack Tupper, 'and then the rain is awful . . . I had to sketch under the canopy of heaven without a hat, and with my umbrella tied over my head.' But it was not only the rain which eroded his principles. 'The fact is, between you and me, that the leaves on the trees I have to paint here appear red, yellow etc. to my eyes; and as of course I know them on that account to be really of a vivid green, it seems rather annoying that I cannot do them so: my subject shrieking aloud for Spring.'[24]

When the picture on which he was working was finally completed in 1872 it was in a totally different idiom, and the trees were indeed green (Plate 24). His failure to cope with the reality of the Kent countryside on its own terms is both a reflection of his artistic inadequacy, and an index of his willingness to abandon the principles and ideals that had motivated the original Brotherhood.

23 William Holman Hunt
*Valentine Rescuing
Sylvia from Proteus*
1851

24 *The Bower Meadow*
1850-72

Colour 6 *Carlisle Wall* 1853

Colour 7 *Dante's Vision of Rachel and Leah* 1855

25 *The Passover in the Holy Family—Gathering Bitter Herbs* 1855-6

26 *Mary in the House of St John* 1858

28 *The Annunciation* 1861

27 *St John Comforting the Virgin at the Foot of the Cross c.* 1857

3

The Annunciation failed to sell, not surprisingly, perhaps, in view of its critical reception, and Rossetti, alarmed by the implications, decided that he should change his subject matter. In fact he was to continue to paint religious pictures throughout the 1850s and 1860s (Plates 25-8, Colour Plate 3), in spite of his own atheism. These include one of the finest of all his paintings, the great *Seed of David* altarpiece in the newly restored Cathedral of Llandaff (Colour Plate 17). But these pictures were the exception and usually a response to specific commissions which demanded religious subjects.

In an undated letter to his aunt of about this period he laments that his pictures appear to be 'not for the market', and describes a painting that he is now beginning, the subject of which is taken from Browning, which he has 'pitched upon principally for its presumptive saleableness.'[1] The painting was to be large ($7\frac{1}{2}$ ft by 4 ft) and included over thirty figures. Taken from Browning's *Pippa Passes* it was indeed well chosen for its 'saleableness' concerning as it did the hopeless and unrequited love of a page for his queen. The page sings outside while the queen's hair is combed within (Plate 29):

> 'Hist' said Kate the Queen
> But 'oh' cried the maiden binding her tresses,
> ''Tis only a page that carols unseen
> Crumbling your hounds their messes
> Fitting your hawks their jesses.'

Technically it was far too ambitious an undertaking for the young and inexperienced artist who soon abandoned it, and all that remains is a small version, murkily painted and in poor condition, though retaining a certain poignant expressiveness in the tortured pose of the page and the matter-of-fact and unidealized representation of the queen, which counterpoints and in some degree transcends the class barriers between the two which could in other hands have made the picture merely ridiculous.

'*Hist' said Kate the Queen* was not in fact Rossetti's first painting from Browning, for in the autumn of 1849 while painting *The Annunciation* he had done a small watercolour called *The Laboratory* (Plate 30), the bright colours and murderous subject matter of which anticipate something of the drama and jewel-like richness of his paintings of the 1850s. It is another court scene, but the lady has been jilted by her noble lover and has visited the apothecary to obtain poison to wreak feudal revenge on her rival. Her payment to the apothecary—sexual—was equally feudal.

When in the autumn of 1849 he was completing *The Annunciation*, and had just finished *The Laboratory* with which it forms so marked a contrast, the short-lived journal of the Pre-Raphaelite Brotherhood, *The Germ*, subtitled 'Thoughts Towards Nature in Poetry, Literature and Art' was founded. Only four issues appeared and the sales were derisory in spite of indulgent reviews and more than ordinarily interesting contents: poems and etchings of high quality, essays and articles of lesser but by no means negligible importance. But the single most important and interesting article in any of the four issues is the story 'Hand and Soul' which Rossetti contributed to the first. It was written one night in December 1849 'chiefly in some five hours after midnight' recalled William Michael. He was contemplating, presumably, the possibility that no one would want to buy the ascetic and unsold *Annunciation* while some of his friends had highly praised the worldly and romantic *Laboratory*. At the same time he was planning '*Hist' said Kate the Queen*, and 'Hand and Soul' should surely be seen as an attempt, however muddled and ill thought-out, to formulate an aesthetic credo.

29 *'Hist!' said Kate the Queen* 1851

30 *The Laboratory* 1849

It is an account of the life of an imaginary thirteenth-century painter from Arezzo called Chiaro dell'Erma. In form it is confusing since some of it is written in the style of a popular biography where the author shares the inmost thoughts of his subject, while other portions are laden with pseudo-academic mumbo-jumbo—references to the researches of 'Dr Aemmster' of Dresden, the 'new catalogue' of the collection in the Pitti Gallery at Florence and so on. The effect is to give a spurious but superficially convincing authenticity to what is in fact a fairy-tale biography—but one with which Rossetti himself quite clearly identifies strongly.

Chiaro conceives art 'almost as it were for himself, and loving it deeply, he endeavoured from early boyhood towards the imitation of any objects offered in nature. The extreme longing after a visible embodiment of his thoughts strengthened as his years increased, more even than his sinews or the blood of his life; until he would feel faint in sunsets, and at the sight of stately persons.'[2] He resolves to become the pupil of Giunta Pisano (an indirect reference to the Pisano brothers who effectively created modern sculpture in Pisa during the last decades of the thirteenth century), but soon abandons his mentor to work on his own. The parallels with Rossetti's own life are only too obvious. Moreover 'women loved Chiaro; for . . . he was well favoured and very manly . . .', but fearing artistic rivals he forsook the pleasures of the world, and spent his whole time at his easel painting 'only living entirely to himself'. Here, perhaps, the wish-fulfilment has begun. For Chiaro lives in austere solitude by the Church of San Rocco, listening to the chanting of the mass through the window of his room, a room which contained apart from 'the matters of his art and a very few books' only 'a small consecrated image of St Mary Virgin wrought out of silver, before which stood always, in summer time, a glass containing a lily and a rose'. Though this is 1849 already we are almost in the absurd *fin de siècle* fantasy world of Huysmans' *A Rebours*.

Chiaro worked all day in his room and having achieved worldly success but remaining spiritually unfulfilled he resolved 'to put his hand to no other works, but only to such as had for their end the presentment of some moral greatness', and these pictures were not to deal with the 'actions and passions of human life' but 'cold symbolism and abstract impersonation'. However, they were a failure, 'laboured, cold and unemphatic'.

Lamenting his state in a fever one day—'Fame failed me, faith failed me'—Chiaro beheld a vision of a woman who said 'I am an image, Chiaro, of thine own soul within thee . . . Fame sufficed not, for that thou didst seek fame: seek thine own conscience (not thy mind's conscience, but thine heart's) and all shall approve and suffice . . . Thou has said that faith failed thee . . . But who bad thee [choose] between love and faith? Wouldst thou sift the warm breeze from the sun that quickens it?' Finally she told Chiaro to paint her, which he did and 'while he worked his face grew solemn with knowledge'.

It is certainly not stretching the evidence too far to see the story as Rossetti's (perhaps only half-conscious) attempt to justify his incipient rejection of the constrictions of the Pre-Raphaelite creed as interpreted by Hunt, in favour of those paintings of the imagination, of love, and of the artist's (or his patron's) subjectivity which were to an increasing degree to occupy most of the rest of his life.

But Rossetti's attempt to abandon paintings of 'cold symbolism and abstract impersonation' which 'had for their end the presentment of some moral greatness' was to be only partially successful. Certainly his work over the next decade concerned itself substantially with the 'actions and passions of human life' and aspirations to 'moral greatness' ceased to trouble him. But by 1870 there was to be no artist in England painting with a symbolism colder or more abstracted, and while the paintings were still concerned with passion, if not action, the passion had become scarcely human or real in its reference.

The idea of a portrait of a woman representing the soul of the artist is objectively ludicrous, as Rossetti was well aware, so we should not expect to find in his own œuvre any paintings that can be remotely accredited as such. Indeed he failed to complete an etching of Chiaro painting his soul which had been planned as an illustration to the story. There are nonetheless a number of paintings and drawings of single female figures that he produced through the next fifteen years, most of them of the girl who was later to become his wife, Elizabeth Siddal, which carry an emotional charge and are of a quasi-religious intensity that is certainly sufficient to justify our designating some of them as 'figura mistica' as Rossetti imagined Chiaro's picture to be catalogued in the Pitti Gallery (Colour Plate 4, Plates 31, 34, 41). The culmination of this theme was perhaps achieved in 1864 with the first version of *Beata Beatrix* (Colour Plate 18).

Elizabeth Siddal was a girl of quite remarkable beauty with whom Rossetti fell totally in love. Already obsessed by the life and writings of Dante his namesake, it would have been surprising if he had not responded positively to a girl who seemed ideally suited to become his own Beatrice. Discovered one day late in 1850 by Rossetti's friend Walter Deverell in a milliner's shop off Leicester Square she was soon sitting for all the Brotherhood and their friends as well. But after 1851 she only sat to Rossetti with whom she developed an increasingly close

31 *The Damsel of the Sanct Grael* 1857

33 *Elizabeth Siddal* 1854

32 *Elizabeth Siddal*

34 *Elizabeth Siddal* 1854

35 *Elizabeth Siddal* 1854

36 *Elizabeth Siddal*

37 *Elizabeth Siddal* 1854

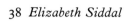

38 *Elizabeth Siddal*

39 *Elizabeth Siddal* 1852

relationship, and from whose paintings of the next ten years her features are seldom absent. We know what she looked like, both from her presence as model in a dozen or more paintings, and also from the large number of surviving pencil and pen and ink drawings and handful of watercolour portraits which Rossetti made of her over the years until her death in 1862 (Plates 32-43). Extraordinarily moving and poignant as these drawings are, and I would argue that taken together they comprise Rossetti's most individual and personal artistic achievement, without precedent or parallel, they still leave Lizzie's character an enigma, and the exact nature of their relationship a puzzle.[3] That Rossetti's drawings do not exaggerate or distort her beauty is clear when we consider contemporary paintings or descriptions of her by others: 'Tall, finely formed, with a lofty neck and regular yet somewhat uncommon features, greenish blue unsparkling eyes, large perfect eyelids, brilliant complexion, and a lavish wealth of coppery golden hair'.[4] But she was consumptive and her health was to become a constant cause of concern. The frail and melancholy personality that so many of Rossetti's obsessive drawings evoke was touchingly characterized by Madox Brown who noted in his diary, 'Called on Dante Rossetti. Saw Miss Siddal looking thinner and more deathlike and more beautiful and more ragged than ever . . . Gabriel . . . drawing wonderful and lovely Guggums [her nickname] one after another, each one a fresh charm, each one stamped with immortality' . . . '[Rossetti] showed me a drawer full of "Guggums", God knows how many . . . it is like a monomania with him. Many of them are matchless in beauty.'[5] One cannot help relating the interminably unhappy love affair and the pathos of the beautiful yet melancholic and fatally ill Lizzie to the dominant features of the paintings that Rossetti was to produce through the 1850s. In November 1852 he took rooms by Blackfriars Bridge, and the pair of them lived together there, painting and writing but seldom leaving town, and seeing a diminishing circle of friends less and less often (Plate 44). Lizzie's own work, though almost totally derivative from Rossetti's, is not without interest. If her poems are simplistically pathetic and self-pitying, some of her paintings demonstrate a robustly romantic choice of subject (Plate 45) and a facility with imaginary medievalisms that easily matches Rossetti's. It is, however, practically impossible to disentangle their mutual shares of many pictures where we may suspect that Rossetti was largely responsible for the design, while others like the *Quest of the Holy Grail* (Colour Plate 5) were quite explicitly shared achievements with the inscription 'EES inv. EES & DGR del'. Together Rossetti and his 'meek unconscious dove'[6]

40 *Elizabeth Siddal*

41 *Elizabeth Siddal*

42 *Elizabeth Siddal* 1850-65

43 *Elizabeth Siddal*

44 *D. G. Rossetti Sitting to Elizabeth Siddal* 1853

46 *St Cecilia* 1856-7

47 Study for woodcut of *St Cecilia* 1856-7

45 Elizabeth Siddal *Clerk Sanders* 1857

Dante G Rossetti to his friend Alex Munro

48 *Paolo and Francesca c.* 1855

49 *The Ballad of Fair Annie c.* 1855

50 *La Belle Dame sans Merci c.* 1855

51 *Dante Drawing an Angel on the First Anniversary of the Death of Beatrice* 1853

gradually fashioned a private dream world, a world articulated by the romances of Malory and poems of Dante, a world in which love was pervasive, but blighted by the certainty of failure and the inevitability of imminent death, and this claustrophobic doom-laden world is expressed in painting after painting of embracing, kissing, parting or lamenting lovers (Plates 46-51, Colour Plates 6, 7).

They are pictures which it is easy to mock for their anachronism, and their occasional awkwardnesses, sometimes deliberate and sometimes not. They are paintings which it is easy to enjoy and respond to for their sentimental and universal reference, and their colourful appeal. But if unfulfilled love and inevitable death are the two great tragedies of the human condition that no possible forms of social arrangement can control, we must accept that in tackling such a series of paintings Rossetti was not totally abdicating from life and its struggles, nor yet succumbing to the fetish of form which was later to exercise so deadening an influence on his art.

And while this stream of mystically intense and obsessively personal yet simultaneously universal small watercolours was being painted, Rossetti was still engaged on various projects which had a much more direct relation to the social realities and artistic developments which had given birth to the Pre-Raphaelite Brotherhood.

The Annunciation had been unsold in 1850, and though its hostile reception led Rossetti to refuse to exhibit again in public until 1857 and thereafter only very sparingly,[7] he nonetheless continued to work on *The Annunciation* and to try to sell it. He refused to exhibit it because of its 'peculiarity', being anxious to avoid the stigma of exhibiting an unsold picture when still worried about his reputation and consequent future financial prospects.[8] Nonetheless Rossetti was able at last to sell it for £50 to a Protestant shipping agent from Belfast, Francis MacCracken—'this blessed afternoon the blessed white eye sore will be finished'. 'You have heard, I believe, that I have got rid of [it] to an Irish maniac.'[9] Little is known, sadly, of MacCracken who had already bought pictures by Hunt and Brown which he was shortly to re-sell at a profit. He was probably buying *The Annunciation* as a speculation too, and certainly Rossetti treated him with ill-concealed contempt. This disdain for his patrons was not, however, greatly affected by their motives, and he was to become equally shameless in his dealings with close friends.

MacCracken, however, was a gift horse not to be ignored, and Rossetti was soon selling him watercolours for £35-50 which he had been happy to sell previously for £12 or £15.[10] Moreover he received a commission for £150 to paint another picture from scratch, and when his first suggestion of *The Virgin in the House of St John* had been turned down by MacCracken (presumably on religious grounds, as he had already had considerable problems in Ulster with *The Annunciation* on this score), Rossetti determined to paint a picture from modern life. *Found* (Colour Plate 8), 'the town subject', 'the calf picture' as Rossetti used to call it, was never finished though in 1881 only a year before his death he wrote to Janey Morris that, 'the eternal *Found* picture is really getting done, the figures close upon finish.'[11]

Not only did *Found* preoccupy Rossetti right until his death, it also echoed a concern that he had voiced and illustrated from his earliest years, and that pervaded Victorian life and thought with extraordinary ubiquity around the years of the mid-century: the theme of the 'fallen woman'. Even now the world of Victorian sexuality is curiously opaque to us, partly because of our own inhibitions and preconceptions, but even more so because of the extraordinary conventions, beliefs and pressures of the time.[12] To a degree Rossetti shared these inhibitions but the scatalogical sonnets that he wrote in Paris in 1849,[13] the unconventional nature of his relationship with Elizabeth Siddal, his subsequently promiscuous liaisons in the 1860s, and the erotic and eccentric tastes which he shared with Swinburne,[14] all indicate a relaxed approach to sexuality and sexual relations. In 1847 he had written a poem 'Jenny':

> Lazy, laughing languid Jenny
> Fond of a kiss and fond of a guinea,

which recounts the reverie of a lover with a sleeping prostitute as dawn approaches, and which Rossetti clearly had in mind when composing *Found*:

> When wealth and health slipped past, you stare
> Along the streets alone, and there,
> Round the long park, across the bridge
> The cold lamps at the pavement's edge
> Wind on together and apart,
> A fiery serpent for your heart.
> And there's an early waggon drawn
> To market, and some sheep that jog
> Bleating before a barking dog.
> And the old streets come peering through
> Another night that London knew
> And all as ghostlike as the lamps.

★   ★   ★

Yesterday's rose now droops forlorn
But dies not yet this summer morn.

Another possible source was a somewhat similar poem 'Rosabell' by Rossetti's friend William Bell Scott, while Rossetti himself appended a sonnet to the frame making the subject quite explicit, and inscribed the earliest of the complete studies for the picture (Plate 52) with the legend from Jeremiah 2:2, which his sister had found for him, 'I remember thee,—the kindness of thy youth, the love of thy betrothal.'

But the theme of the returned lover reproaching the infidelity of his one-time companion is a timeless one and it is not necessary or possible to identify the exact prototype. More interesting is that during the gestation of this picture in 1853 both Holman Hunt and Madox Brown were simultaneously engaged on paintings from modern life. Madox Brown's *Work* (Manchester City Art Gallery) and Hunt's *Awakening Conscience* (Private Collection) both have clear affinities to *Found*, and all three, as Virginia Surtees has pointed out,[15] could be taken directly from the pages of Henry Mayhew's *London Labour and the London Poor* which had first appeared in the *Morning Chronicle* in 1849-50, and was continued in a series of privately published pamphlets in 1851-2 after Mayhew tired of the predictable editorial tampering on the 'respectable' *Morning Chronicle*. They had had a devastating impact on the sensibilities of many contemporaries— they provide, wrote Thackeray, 'a picture of human life so wonderful, so awful, so piteous and pathetic, so exciting and terrible, that readers of romances own they never read anything like to it'. [16] One subsection of the chapter on prostitution describes 'Park Women':

Park women . . . are those degraded creatures, utterly lost to all sense of shame, who wander about the paths most frequented after nightfall in the parks, and consent to any species of humiliation for the sake of acquiring a few shillings. You may meet them in Hyde Park . . . till the gates are closed. In the Green Park, in what is called The Mall . . . you may see these low wretches walking about sometimes with men, more generally alone, often early in the morning. . . . The unfortunate women that form this despicable class have in some cases been well off and have been reduced to their present condition by a variety of circumstances . . . I questioned one . . . and she [replied] 'I have not always been what I am now. Twenty years ago I was in a very different position . . . I am the daughter of a curate in Gloucestershire . . . my mother educated me at home . . . I saw that the limited resources of my parents would not allow them

I remember thee : the kindness of thy youth, the love of thy betrothal.

52 Study for *Found* 1853

"I remember thee; the kindness of thy youth, the love of thy betrothal." *Jerem. II.2.*

Found

53 Study for *Found* c. 1855

54 & 55 Studies for *Found c.* 1859-61

56 Study for *Found c.* 1860

to maintain me at home without seriously impairing their resources, and I proposed that I should go out as a governess . . . Then I was very pretty. I may say so without vanity or ostentation for I had many admirers among whom I numbered the only son of the people in whose home I lived . . . My life might have been very happy if an unfortunate attachment to me had not sprung up in the young man . . . which attachment I can never sufficiently regret was reciprocated by myself . . .'[17]

And so on. Rossetti is not illustrating Mayhew, but the parallel is fairly close, and it is scarcely conceivable that he was uninfluenced by his writings.

The painting is an important statement of Rossetti's essentially humanistic and liberal involvement in the human tragedy. He was a great admirer of Elizabeth Gaskell[18] whose *Mary Barton* is by far the most powerfully critical and realistic of the socially concerned novels of the 1840s. He sympathized with the struggles of the Irish to liberate themselves from English oppression and actively agitated (with Madox Brown and Swinburne) on behalf of the five Fenians hanged at Manchester in November 1867 for the alleged murder of a policeman.[19] Moreover he had much earlier encouraged his friend Walter Deverell to paint *The Irish Vagrants* (Johannesburg Art Gallery) which shows a family of desperately poor and starving Irish sitting by the roadside at harvest-time while in the background harvesters are at work in the fields, and a haughtily patrician lady (presumably the local landowner) rides by, ignoring the pleas of the small children. 'Rossetti [was of the] opinion that . . . as the subject was so good and important I had better paint it on a larger scale',[20] noted Deverell. This sympathetic view of the Irish problem was a significant and by any standards creditable one to take publicly at a time when most Englishmen would have been more likely to have shared Thomas Carlyle's view that 'Ireland is like a half-starved rat that crosses the path of an elephant. What must the elephant do? Squelch it—by heavens—squelch it!'

Rossetti probably devoted more of his life to *Found* than to any other single picture. Eighteen studies for it and a replica (mainly painted by H. Treffry Dunn) survive, and it occupied him substantially in 1854, 1861, 1862, 1870 and 1880-1 (Plates 52-56). Madox Brown records the pains he took over the calf, painting it 'like Albert Dürer, hair by hair'.[20] But it was not the only picture that he painted on the theme, and it is important to bear in mind the difficulty he had in selling *Found* when we consider the stylistic changes that began to take place in his art around 1857. *Hesterna Rosa* (Yesterday's

Quoth tongue of neither maid nor wife
  To heart of neither wife nor maid:
"Lead we not here a jolly life
  Betwixt the shine and shade?"

Quoth heart of neither maid nor wife
  To tongue of neither wife nor maid:
"Then wag'st, but I am worn with th[?]
  And feel like flowers that fade."

57 *Hesterna Rosa* 1853

58 *The Gate of Memory c.* 1857

Rose) (Plate 57) dates from 1850, though the only surviving drawing is dated 1853, and represents the morning after of two lovers with their mistresses. It is based on Elena's song from Henry Taylor's currently popular verse play *Philip van Artevelde*. The lonely dismay and despair of one of the girls (an impression heightened by the contrast between the angelic child playing the lute on the left and the ape scratching itself on the right) is perhaps echoed in *The Gate of Memory* (Plate 58) of 1857 where a single prostitute at dusk watches a group of children playing, and recognizes herself as she once was in the form of the innocent, flower-crowned child on the left. This painting is quite explicitly based on Bell Scott's 'Rosabell', but before going on to consider Rossetti's difficulties with his patrons over these subjects it is perhaps as well to return to 'Jenny' where Rossetti makes quite clear the basis of the degradation which these pictures represent, and the sexist class indifference which has promoted the tragedies of their protagonists:

> What has man done here? How atone,
> Great God for this which man has done?
> And for the body and the soul which by
> Man's pitiless doom must now comply
> With lifelong hell, what lullaby
> Of sweet forgetful second birth
> Remains?

4

Found had been commissioned for £150 as a speculation by MacCracken, who probably found the down-to-earth subject matter no disadvantage. Progress, however, was so slow that the contract lapsed, and it was not until six years later, in 1859, that Rossetti was able to write to Madox Brown that another patron was interested. 'The sainted Leathart [a Newcastle lead merchant] seems to project giving me a larger commission but after all funks the calf picture for the usual reason.'[1] The reason, of course, was the subject, which was becoming increasingly unacceptable in conventional bourgeois circles as the 1850s progressed and the heyday of cosy, insulated, hypocritical, domestic middle-class virtue approached. Leathart, however, was extremely keen to acquire a work by Rossetti and within a couple of weeks had agreed to recommission *Found* for £350. The painting dragged on interminably, however, and in 1867 Rossetti paid Leathart back the money that he had been advanced for it, only to get it recommissioned again two years later for £800 by William Graham, a member of Parliament from Glasgow, who eventually acquired it, incomplete, on Rossetti's death in 1882.

The history of the commission demonstrates admirably both Rossetti's dilatoriness, and his shrewd business sense. Patrons existed to be exploited so far as he was concerned and though he was a highly successful manipulator of this relationship, it, like all forms of social intercourse and control, had a dialectical element which gradually deprived his own work of the urgency, realism and personality which are so impressive in his early works. The position of the artist in the market place had become critical by the middle years of the nineteenth century as the relatively consistent and responsible aristocratic patronage began to decline, and its place was taken by a much more ruthless and capriciously irresponsible free market where the only consideration became the value or desirability of the particular picture under consideration, and the artist's life or work as a totality counted for little or nothing. The situation has become progressively worse since then, but whatever the most desirable relationship between artist and patron (and by extension society as a whole) may be, it is certainly not that which Rossetti established and manipulated so successfully (in financial terms) to his own advantage. The expropriation of his patrons went hand in hand with the alienation of his own art. Though he reversed the usual domination of living labour power by dead labour power (i.e. the control of the work of the living by the objectified labour of the past which has been appropriated in the form of capital by the well to do) he succeeded only in distorting, and some might argue destroying, his own talents.

Rossetti affected to feel nothing but contempt for his patrons: 'I understand they have *plenty of tin to begin with*, and I suppose would of course pay well,' he wrote to Madox Brown in 1853,[2] '. . . the chief thing is to *lay it on* thick as to payment, as I believe they really have tin. T is, of course, an ass, and should on principle be treated with ignominy.' And he was equally scathing about the man who more than anyone else first established his art on a firm economic base by both publicly defending the Pre-Raphaelites and privately buying, and advising others to buy, Rossetti's work—John Ruskin. 'Ruskin . . . the other day wrote me an incredible letter . . . remaining mine respectfully (!!) and wanting to call. I of course stroked him down in my answer, and yesterday he came. His manner was more agreeable than I had always expected, but in person he is an absolute Guy—worse than Patmore.

'However he seems in a mood to make my fortune.'[3]

The same year, 1854, in the published version of some lectures on art Ruskin wrote, 'I question whether even the greatest men of old times possessed more invention than either Millais or Rossetti',[4] and as William Rossetti observed, 'a word from Ruskin will do more to attract notice to merit as yet unadmitted than anything else whatever.'[5] This quite unprecedented praise was followed up by much advice, generosity, and many individual commissions. 'Amongst all the painters I know, you on the whole have the greatest genius. . . . I really do *covet* your drawings as much as I covet Turner's, only it is useless self-indulgence to buy Turner's, and useful self-indulgence to buy yours,' wrote Ruskin in 1855.[6] Rossetti's response in letters to his friends was to refer derisively to Ruskin 'beginning to bear fruit',[7] and generally to raise his prices and reduce his output, so that during 1854 and the early part of 1855 he produced scarcely any work.

Rossetti's mercenary skills and astute control of the market are borne out by much contemporary comment, and most tellingly, perhaps, by his brother William:

> There was no better hand at a bargain. . . . My brother understood how far he could go—so far he went; and having fixed the terms he knew how to stick by them, unregardful of dubiety or demur. . . . A business man who is a picture buyer . . . has his weak side, and, so far as his relation to art goes, he feels it is a privilege to be made free of the art-precincts, and promoted into the intimacy of a great or distinguished painter. He is apt to find the world of art much more entertaining than the world of commerce; and while pluming himself about having converse with persons whose names are in all men's mouths he can still feel that, in a certain sense, he himself "rules the roost" as all these fine performances would collapse without a purchaser to sustain them. No one knew this better than Rossetti. His net was spread in the sight, but not too obviously in the sight, of several birds.[8]

William acutely defines the way in which Rossetti would manipulate his market. The changing social position of the artist by which he was becoming a man different from other men, a man not involved in or implicated by the realities of everyday life, and not expected to behave in a necessarily decent or rational way, gave great opportunities to the successful. It gave them the freedom to control the demand for their work as well as the supply of it. With characteristic even-handedness the market also gave the less successful ever greater freedom to starve, as the litter of impoverished artists whose lives are such a familiar feature of the history of art after the mid-nineteenth century bears witness.

The increasing domination of market forces and the commoditization of art had interesting intellectual and semantic overtones. By and large the aesthetic response to it of Rossetti and his contemporaries was to lapse into ever more formalized exercises and increasingly to judge and justify what they did by self-consistent but circular arguments culminating in the doctrine of art for art's sake which was even now around 1860 beginning to be developed by Swinburne, Pater and others. This attitude was in turn justified by reference to a 'philistine' society which was antipathetic to true art. But 'philistinism' had previously meant something quite different. In the eighteenth century 'philistinism' had been the label given to resignation before the degradation of life, and against which Diderot, Lessing, Goethe and Rousseau had struggled. This struggle effectively culminated in the French Revolution, but in the reaction to this, and particularly in the mid-nineteenth century, 'philistinism' came to be re-defined as 'a stupid response to genuine art'.[9] This, of course, was a total reversal of meaning, for it was essentially the aesthetic rejection of life, or pseudo-protest against it, which represented the capitulation to degrading reality.[10]

Rossetti thus participated most directly in the establishment of forms of aesthetic practice, trade and self-justification which were ultimately to have the most disastrous results in terms of responsibility ignored, genius neglected and meretricious trivia exalted. The repercussions of these developments are still very much with us, and though Rossetti's actual responsibility for the forms or the direction which resulted was no greater than that of many other individuals, his position at a focal point of the change had profound consequences for his own art.

Essentially the changes in his own art that were to take place as a result of his relations with his patrons were firstly an increasing tendency to subordinate his creativity by repeating themes that had already proved popular with clients, and secondly to adopt not the more searching, studied and various style that (for example) makes all Cézanne's studies of Mont Sainte Victoire, or Turner's of Norham Castle, of equal or increasing interest as visual explorations, but to lapse increasingly into a florid, hasty and sometimes only passably competent mannerism that betrays both the shallowness of his inspiration, and the technical improficiency which his originality, commitment and pictorially expressed personality had hitherto transcended.

But though he began his first substantial replica in 1855 (*Beatrice Meeting Dante at a Wedding Feast Denies him her Salutation*— ironically for Ruskin, now in the Ashmolean Museum, Oxford) Rossetti still achieved three unequivocally impressive sequences of painting in the course of the next few years.

Colour 9 *Arthur's Tomb* 1855

Colour 10 *Sir Launcelot's Vision of the Sanc Grael* 1857

Colour 11 *How Sir Galahad, Sir Bors and Sir Percival were fed with the Sanc Grael; but Sir Percival's sister Died by the Way* 1864

Colour 12 *The Tune of Seven Towers* 1857

In 1857 Rossetti together with various others undertook to paint a fresco cycle in the newly built debating hall (now the library) of the Oxford University Union. The architect, Woodward, was a friend of Rossetti's, and Ruskin had persuasively argued that new buildings might be appropriately decorated by young artists giving their services for nothing. When invited to participate by two young admirers of his at Oxford, William Morris and Edward Burne-Jones, Rossetti found the challenge irresistible, and having persuaded his fellow painters to reject the portentous philosophic subjects such as 'Newton Gathering Pebbles on the Ocean of Truth' which had been proposed by the somewhat self-consciously serious students, they set to work on a series of designs taken from Malory's *Morte D'Arthur*.

As well as meeting Morris and Burne-Jones, it was at Oxford that Rossetti first met Swinburne (Plate 59) with whom he established a long lasting and mutually important friendship. Then only twenty, but already a brilliantly original lyricist, a republican, a revolutionary, and shortly to leave the University in order to avoid being expelled, Swinburne was immediately attracted by and attractive to the older poet. They had much in common, and together with Morris, Burne-Jones, and their three fellow artists—Arthur Hughes, Hungerford Pollen and Val Prinsep—they passed a wild and indulgent summer. 'The months that I spent at Oxford I have always considered as among the most delightful of a life which has certainly not been without enjoyment,' wrote Prinsep in 1904.[11] Another contemporary observer later recalled the event: 'A merry, rollicking set they were: I was working daily in the library, which at that time opened into the gallery of the new room, and heard their laughter and song, and jokes, and the volleys of soda-water corks; for this innutrient fluid was furnished to them without stint at the Society's expense, and the bill from the Star Hotel, close by, amazed the Treasurer.'[12]

Although in some respects the portrait of Rossetti which this book is attempting to paint is not an altogether attractive one in personal terms, it would not do to neglect or ignore the affection and regard in which he was held by his friends. 'No one in this world ever owed so much to another as I do to you,' wrote Burne-Jones to him in 1877, while in 1894 to F.G. Stephens who was then writing his book on Rossetti he wrote that he had 'worshipped Gabriel more than anyone who ever lived'. 'At Oxford,' recalled Burne-Jones' widow Georgiana, 'Gabriel was in his glory and Edward [Burne-Jones] and Morris sat at his feet and rejoiced in the light—and they were so beautiful . . .'

Before the Oxford Union commission, Arthurian legend had already provided Rossetti with the inspiration for one astonishingly

Colour 13 *The Chapel before the Lists* 1857

Colour 14 *St Catherine* 1857

intense little watercolour. *Arthur's Tomb*, of 1855 (Colour Plate 9), was done for Ruskin, and shows Lancelot and Guinevere parting for the last time at Arthur's tomb with Guinevere, inhibited by the setting, refusing to kiss her lover. But the Oxford Murals were the first pictures actually to illustrate incidents recorded by Malory. Unfortunately they were painted 'in thin distemper upon a coat of whitewash applied to an ordinary brick wall',[13] and no sooner were they applied than they began to fade. Rossetti was allocated two bays to decorate, but he only began one (*Sir Launcelot's Vision of the Sanc Grael*) which he failed to complete though 'Ruskin with money inducements, and others independently, pressed him to return, but without avail.'[14] Nonetheless the composition is preserved (Colour Plate 10, Plates 60-62) and shows a remarkably successful integration of the picture surface into its architectural setting. 'My own subject', he wrote, 'is Sir Launcelot prevented by his sins from entering the chapel of the San Grail. He has fallen asleep before the shrine full of angels, and between him and it rises in his dream the image of Queen Guinevere the cause of all. She stands gazing at him with her arms extended in the branches of an apple tree.'[15] The second, unexecuted, design, *The Attainment of the Sanc Grael*, is also recorded in drawings (Plate 63) and was later carried out in a watercolour version (Colour Plate 11) slightly modified to take account of the absence of window apertures.

Also at Oxford in the summer of 1857 appeared the second of the two women who were to haunt Rossetti throughout his life. Jane Burden was the seventeen-year-old daughter of a groom, and Rossetti and his friends first saw her one night at the theatre. William Rossetti described her:

Her face was at once tragic, mystic, passionate, calm, beautiful and gracious—a face for a sculptor and a face for a painter—a face solitary in England and not at all like that of an Englishwoman, but rather of an Ionian Greek. It was not a face for that large class of English people who only take to the 'pretty' and not to the beautiful or superb. Her complexion was dark and pale, her eyes a deep penetrating grey, her massive wealth of hair gorgeously rippled, and tending to black, yet not without some deep-sunken glow.[16]

It seems probable that Rossetti immediately incorporated her portrait into one of the studies that he was doing for the Union Murals (Plate 60), though Elizabeth Siddal's features are clearly visible in others (Plate 62). Certainly he drew her in Oxford that October (Plate 64), and although she was to marry Morris two years later in 1859, Rossetti's affection, and, we may presume, love for her provided him

Colour 16 *Sir Galahad at the Ruined Chapel* 1859

63 Study for *The Attainment of the Sanc Grael* 1857

64 *Jane Morris* 1857

Colour 17 *The Seed of David* (central panel) 1858-64

Colour 18 *Beata Beatrix* 1864

65 William Morris *Queen Guinevere* 1858

with such personal artistic stimulus as he needed until the end of his life. Other women sat for him, other women lived with him, but none save the ailing Elizabeth Siddal remotely approached Jane Morris as visual or individual inspiration.

While they were at Oxford together Morris also painted Jane as Guinevere (Plate 65) but so far as Rossetti's own artistic output was concerned, Morris' most immediately important act was to commission or purchase from him no less than five watercolours: *The Blue Closet* (Plate 66), *The Tune of Seven Towers* (Colour Plate 12), *The Damsel of the Sanct Grael* (Plate 31), *The Chapel Before the Lists* (Colour Plate 13) and *The Death of Breuze sans Pitié* (lost). The same year saw the completion of *The Wedding of St George and the Princess Sabra* (Plate 67), *A Christmas Carol* (Plate 68) and *St Catherine* (Colour Plate 14) among other small and highly worked up paintings. Nearly all taken from medieval romances, many from Malory, and nearly all brilliantly coloured jewel-like representations of idealized if often ill-fated love (Colour Plates 15 and 16), they form a remarkable group and represent an unprecedented burst of creativity. 'These chivalric Froissartian themes are quite a passion of mine,' he observed in a letter to Charles Eliot Norton of Harvard who had commissioned another, *Before the Battle* (Colour Plate 15). As Madox Brown was to note, perhaps a little indulgently, in his diary, 'They form an admirable picture of the world of our fathers with its chief character-istics—religion, art, chivalry and love. His forte, and he seems to have found it out, is to be a lyrical painter and poet, and certainly a glorious one.'

Glorious though they were, these paintings lacked the edge that Morris imparted to the medievalizing poems that he published the following year under the title *The Defence of Guinevere*. Two of the poems in this book, 'The Blue Closet' and 'The Tune of the Seven Towers' are directly based on watercolours he bought from Rossetti, and we have Rossetti's word for it that the paintings of the same title preceded them, but these are among the weaker poems in the book. There are others of a haunting melancholy and almost unprecedented brutal realism that Rossetti will certainly have heard Morris read aloud in 1857 and which it is almost inevitable we should think of as one of the inspirations for the sequence of watercolours that ensued— in particular perhaps the superbly modulated 'Haystack in the Floods'—an account of a knight's execution in front of his lover Jehane by his captor Godmar. The taut brutal realism of the execu-tion, in its dripping and dismally plausible setting, is overlain by the tragically inadequate and irrelevant code of honour which brings it

66 *The Blue Closet* 1857

67 *The Wedding of St George and the Princess Sabra* 1857

68 *A Christmas Carol* 1857-8

about. For Jehane's refusal to yield to Godmar, which would save her lover's life, merely ensures that he is executed before Godmar takes her by force.

> With a start
> Up Godmar rose, thrust them apart;
> From Robert's throat he loosed the bounds
> Of silk and mail; with empty hands
> Held out, she stood, and gazed, and saw
> The long bright blade without a flaw
> Glide out from Godmar's sheath, his hand
> In Robert's hair; she saw him bend
> Back Robert's head; she saw him send
> The thin steel down; the blow told well
> Right backward the knight Robert fell
> And moan'd as dogs do being half dead
> Unwitting, as I deem: so then
> Godmar turn'd grinning to his men
> Who ran some five or six and beat
> His head to pieces at their feet.

This savage actuality and commentary on feudal social and personal relations is of course never achieved in Rossetti's medievalizing paintings, but it underlies them, and to many gives an additional poignancy. Certainly Rossetti's medieval dream world was nothing like as gentle, noble or chaste as that of Burne-Jones and his many followers, and he greatly admired Morris' verse. 'When dinner was over', recalled Val Prinsep,

> Rossetti humming to himself as was his wont, rose from the table, and proceeded to curl himself up on the sofa. 'Top', he said, 'read us one of your grinds.' 'No, Gabriel', answered Morris, 'you have heard them all.' 'Never mind', said Rossetti, 'here's Prinsep who has never heard them, and besides they are devilish good.' 'Very well, old chap', growled Morris and . . . began to read in a sing song chant some of the poems afterwards published. . . . To this day, forty years after, I can still recall the scene . . . [it] still seems to haunt me . . .
>
> > Swerve to the left, son Roger, he said
> >   When you catch his eyes through the helmet slit,
> > Swerve to the left then out at his head,
> >   And the Lord God give you joy of it![18]

As Edward Thompson has pointed out, the vivid realism exemplified in the finest poems, 'Sir Peter Harpdon's End', 'The Haystack in the

69 Study for *The Seed of David c.* 1856

Floods' and 'The Defence of Guinevere', itself gives them a claim to be considered as almost 'the last true and uncorrupted works of the Romantic Revolt,'[19] and it is a special irony that their creation should have coincided so closely with the abrupt transition in Rossetti's art of which Morris then had such a high opinion.

This transition cannot be exactly dated, but gradually between 1857 and 1860 a dramatic break occurred. Something of it can be seen in the progress of the work on the altarpiece which Rossetti managed to get the commission for in the newly restored Cathedral of Llandaff outside Cardiff. For though he landed the commission in 1856 and his original design dates from then (Plates 69-71) the final version was not completed till 1864 (Colour Plate 17, Plate 72) and noble though it is, the simplicity and innocence of the earlier picture have quite disappeared.[20] It is the only commission given to any of the Pre-Raphaelites which can really be compared to those of their Italian namesakes, and in terms of composition Rossetti rose to the occasion. The triptych form was sanctioned by ancient practice, and the composition showing in the central panel a symbolic nativity at which a shepherd and a king worship the child, while the two wings portray David (the shepherd who became the king) in each of his roles, has a neat simplicity of reference that might conceivably be thought to echo a fifteenth-century scheme. If it had been painted (as the first watercolour version indicated that it might be) in the style of *The Annunciation* or *The Girlhood of Mary Virgin* it could have been a remarkable picture. In spite of the grotesquely inappropriate 'modern' frame in which it is now mounted it remains an impressive and expressive work, but it is let down by the sombre, almost murky, palette and careless brushwork which were increasingly to characterize Rossetti's art after 1860 as he again took up painting in oils.

He turned to oils for basically commercial reasons—higher prices could be commanded for oil paintings which could also be larger, thus facilitating rapid brushwork, and, again, higher prices. But the other pictures of the late fifties that demonstrate the changing style are not all in oils. Two of them at least are highly elaborated pen and ink drawings of some size: *Sir Launcelot in the Queen's Chamber* (Plate 73) and *Mary Magdalene at the Door of Simon the Pharisee* (Plate 74), which date from 1857 and 1858 respectively. What distinguishes these two drawings from Rossetti's previous work is a certain coarseness of manner, notwithstanding their still meticulously detailed technique. Both are scenes of lives in a state of sexual crisis, and though this is not an entirely new feature in Rossetti's work, some reference to his own personal problems may be present if only unconsciously. The some-

72 Study for *The Seed of David* 1862

73 *Sir Launcelot in the Queen's Chamber* 1857

74 *Mary Magdalene at the Door of Simon the Pharisee* 1858

75 *Bocca Baciata* 1859

what gross and even vulgar treatment of these subjects when seen in the context of what was to follow is something of a milestone, though it was only with the oil painting *Bocca Baciata* ('Kissed Mouth') (Plate 75) of the following year that any of his contemporaries marked the change. A painting of Fanny Cornforth, a girl of generous habits whom Rossetti had recently met, it is the prototype of his output over the ensuing twenty-three years until his death. The feeling is still melancholy but no allusion to reality in material, historical or ideological form is made. The sitter is alone, with no point of reference to the world or anyone other than the viewer (or owner) except sometimes for a symbolic piece of fruit or rich array of draperies or flowers. The picture means what we wish to read into it. In this case it is not a great deal more than a portrait of Fanny with a background of marigolds and an apple, but gradually the paintings of this type take on an almost mechanical and iconic quality as the world and its problems are left further and further behind. Gradually the small, angular and medievalized figures are replaced by sombre, languorous and humourless ladies whose distinguishing features are their columnar necks, their curling lips, their plentiful dark hair and their deeply private and inscrutable sorrows which the observer is invited to consider, and even share, but as to whose nature no clue is usually provided. The titles of the pictures are often Italian, and the background to the ladies usually consists of dense swirling arabesques of a proto-*art nouveau* nature, either embroidered on damask as a pattern, or provided naturally by smoke, hair, foliage or, occasionally, companion figures.

Arthur Hughes was enchanted. He wrote to William Allingham, 'Rossetti has lately finished a most beautiful head . . . such a superb thing, so awfully lovely. Boyce has bought it and will I expect kiss the dear thing's lips away before you come over to see it.'[21] Boyce also thought it 'splendid' and noted in his diary that 'Stanhope . . . admired it as greatly as I did.'[22] Holman Hunt, predictably perhaps, was appalled by its voluptuousness. He wrote to a friend,

> Most people admire it very much and speak to me of it as a triumph of our school. I have strong prejudices and may be influenced by them . . . [but] I will not scruple to say that it impresses me as very remarkable in power of execution—but still more remarkable for gross sensuality of a revolting kind, peculiar to foreign prints that would scarcely pass our English Custom House from France even after the establishment of the most liberal conditions of Free Trade. I would not speak so unreservedly of it were it not that I see Rossetti is advocating as a principle mere gratification of the eye and, if any

76 *St George and the Dragon* 1861-2

77 *The Wedding of St George* 1864

passion at all, the animal passion to be the aim of the art.[23]

We do not need to share Hunt's moralistic prejudices to realize what a departure from the past the picture represented. Rossetti had no doubts. In November he wrote to Bell Scott,

> I have painted a half figure in oil, in doing which I have made an effort to avoid what I know to be a besetting sin of mine and indeed rather common to P.R. painting—that of stippling on the flesh. I have succeeded in quite keeping the niggling process at a distance this time, and am very desirous of painting, whenever I can find leisure and opportunity, various figures of this kind chiefly as studies of rapid flesh painting. I am sure that among the many botherations of a picture where design, drawing, expression and colour have to be thought of all at once (and this perhaps in the focus of the four winds out of doors . . .) one can never do justice even to what faculty of mere painting may be in one . . . I have been struggling in a labyrinth of things it seems impossible to get on with, and things which it seems impossible to begin.[24]

Now he could see a way out of the 'labyrinth', by substituting 'rapid flesh painting' for the 'niggling . . . botherations . . . of P.R. painting, but he did not take it right away. In 1859-60 his relationship with Elizabeth Siddal reached a crisis which resulted in their marriage. But it was almost certainly a step of desperation—a triumph of hope over experience. His poems of the period are full of expressive gloom with a surely personal reference. And although a burst of activity around the time of his marriage produced a group of finely worked up drawings (Plates 76-80) which show him exploring new themes (stained-glass designs for Morris and Company, the elaborately classical, and the humorously anecdotal), the lugubrious *How They Met Themselves* (Plate 81) which shows two lovers in a wood meeting their doubles—according to the *doppelgänger* legend a sure presage of death—seems a strange subject for him to have taken up on his honeymoon, even though it was something he had been working on intermittently since 1851. He also reworked a sketch of Hamlet and Ophelia first composed in 1854, illustrating the moment when Ophelia returns to Hamlet the letters and presents he had given her— a theme of constant interest to him (Plates 82-4).

Hamlet   I did love you once
Ophelia   Indeed my lord, you made me believe so
Hamlet   You should not have believed . . . I loved you not

In 1862 Lizzie died. The evidence is confusing, but it seems more likely than not that she killed herself as a result of her melancholia and

78 *Cassandra* 1861

79 *Dr Johnson at the Mitre* 1860

81 *How They Met Themselves* 1860

82 *Hamlet and Ophelia* 1858

83 *The First Madness of Ophelia* 1864

the increasing pain of her illness. Whether by accident or design the cause of death was an overdose of laudanum. In spite (or perhaps because) of the personal devastation which Rossetti suffered, and the remorse with which he never ceased to reproach himself, Elizabeth Siddal's death provided the personal impetus that was perhaps necessary if the impending changes in his art were to become fully worked out.

84 *Hamlet and Ophelia* 1866

5

As soon as Lizzie died Rossetti left the apartment at Blackfriars Bridge and took a large house on Cheyne Walk in Chelsea at a rent of £100 a year which he shared with Swinburne, George Meredith and his brother William. As a gesture of remorse he had buried in Lizzie's coffin the sole manuscript of his unpublished work of verse, and for the next six years he wrote little. His immediate attention indeed was given over to the furnishing and preparation of his new house.

The descriptions that we have of the style in which Rossetti lived in Cheyne Walk scarcely induce sympathy for his regular pleas of poverty. He must have spent a great deal of money acquiring 'Chinese tables and chairs, Dutch tiles, Flemish and oriental and African curtains and draperies, looking glasses and mirrors of the seventeenth and eighteenth centuries, a chandelier here and another there, and numerous knick knacks of whatever kind'.[1] His particular passion became blue and white china, newly imported in quantities from the Far East, a passion shared and encouraged by many of his changing circle of friends including Whistler and the antique dealer Murray Marks. As well as widening his circle of friendships he installed Fanny Cornforth as his resident housekeeper (Plates 85-8), and for the next few years lived a relatively convivial and cheerful life surrounded by his possessions, his friends and his animals—most notably perhaps his famous wombat (Plates 89-90).

Munby recalls an evening of about this time which conveys something of the flavour:

> I was the first to arrive, and found Dante and his brother William in the large quaint studio, full of great easels and hung with DGR's sketches. . . . While we talked, and Rossetti, looking like a younger Faust in that weird chamber, was nursing his Canadian marmot in his arms the others came in. . . . After a hearty greeting all round we went upstairs to dine in that large and lordly upper chamber with the deep half cylinder alcove, looking out on the river. But the wonderful figured Japanese curtains that line that side of the room were down; pictures and ancient china and grotesque bronzes and black carven furniture relieve the blue wainscot and break up the vast apartment into spaces well arranged and harmonious; and in the midst is the white table, lit by red waxlights in silver candelabra standing on a great antique silver plateau. The glass, the china, are all antique: the dinner elaborate and refined, is handed round by a single female servant; a robust and comely young matron, whose large strong hands, used to serving, contrast with the small hands of her master, used to pictures and to poems.[2]

Among the pictures that Munby noticed may have been the portrait of Esmerelda Bandinelli by Botticelli that Rossetti acquired at about this time.[3] But his own output had diminished.

It was not until 1864 that he produced a major picture which developed the precedent set by *Bocca Baciata*, though *Fair Rosamund* of 1861 (Plate 91) and *Helen of Troy* of 1863 (Kunsthalle, Hamburg) represent experiments in that direction. *Beata Beatrix* (Colour Plate 18), however, represents the fusion of the obsessive image of Elizabeth Siddal with the developing technique of the half or three-quarter length single female figure, painted in oil and pictured in a trance-like state of enchantment. Though begun many years previously it was taken up in 1864 as a form of memorial to his wife, representing the moment when Beatrice, while sitting on her balcony looking over Florence dies and 'is suddenly rapt from Earth to Heaven'.[4]

As well as being a valediction to Elizabeth Siddal it represents her in a more worldly form than had ever been Rossetti's custom before. Though hardly 'saturated with passion [that] baffles description', as

85 *Fanny Cornforth* 1865

86 *Woman Combing her Hair* 1864

87 *Morning Music* 1864

89 *Death of a Wombat* 1869

*I never reared a young Wombat
To glad me with his pin-hole eye,
But when he most was sweet & fat
And tail-less, he was sure to die!*

90 H. Treffry Dunn *Rossetti's Sitting Room
at 16, Cheyne Walk* 1872

91 *Fair Rosamund* 1861

92 *A Fight for a Woman* 1865

F. G. Stephens considered *Bocca Baciata* to have been,[5] it is none-theless worlds away from the asceticism of his earlier portrait drawings or the scenes of courtly love of the 1850s.

It was sold to William Cowper Temple for £315[6]—far more than Rossetti had ever received for a picture before except for the enormous Llandaff altarpiece that he was just completing. Much admired, Rossetti was prevailed upon to paint replicas and he put his hand to no less than six versions before he died, of which the best was commissioned by Graham in 1872—'I have been doing a replica here (of that *Beatrice*)—a beastly job but lucre was the lure.'[7] So much in demand were copies of the picture that Graham had to pay £945 for his.

In spite of his lack of enthusiasm for the copying jobs Rossetti was ready enough to embark on them if necessary to maintain the standard of living to which he was becoming accustomed. It is easy enough to demonstrate the way in which this demand of the market diverted his energies from the creative originality of which he was capable. A more subtle and difficult point to demonstrate is that he could not have satisfied the market with less erotic, formalized and symbolic creations—that is that the specific economic and cultural demands of the 1860s and 1870s combined to destroy the demand for the kind of picture that he had been producing in the 1850s. There is no question that the latter—private, modest and even discreet—were relatively less highly respected by his bourgeois patrons of the 1860s and 1870s, and men like Graham the MP, Rae the Birkenhead banker, Trist the Brighton wine merchant and Leyland the Liverpool shipowner were not interested in acquiring them second-hand even at knock down prices.[8] But in 1865 he did produce two watercolours that bear comparison with his work of ten years earlier (Colour Plate 19, Plate 92). Given the number of men now trying to obtain his paintings and prepared to pay fancy prices for them it is very relevant that these two pictures—the last flowering of his medievalizing romanticism of the 1850s—should have been acquired, one by his friend Boyce for an almost certainly modest sum, while the other (*A Fight for a Woman*) which had been begun for Gambart, the sharpest and most successful art dealer in Europe at the time, was turned down by him as being 'likely to prove unpopular'.[9] In the same year Gambart had bought a very different picture from Rossetti, *The Blue Bower* (Plate 93) for £120 and resold it within weeks to Agnew's for £500.

There could be no doubt about the direction in which the economic tide was flowing, and Rossetti was not going to resist it. His next big picture *The Beloved* (Colour Plate 20) is essentially a splendidly elaborated version of *The Blue Bower* with a somewhat unconvincing and inappropriate but mildly erotic quotation from the Song of Solomon attached.[10] George Rae, the managing director of the North and South Wales Bank, gave him £300 for it, and a few years later bought the not dissimilar *Monna Vanna* (Colour Plate 21).

It would perhaps be helpful to put these sums into some kind of perspective. In the 1850s Rossetti had been usually able to command £30-50 for his small watercolours. For these substantially larger but more loosely and hence rapidly executed oils he was getting about ten times as much. Moreover he was tapping an increasingly rich seam, and by the mid 1870s was able to ask twice as much again—£800 to £1,000 was not at all uncommon. G.H.Fleming has calculated his income for 1866 to exceed £2,000, and £3,000 in 1867.[11] In 1876 he wrote to his mother, 'Would you believe it that my Bank passbook shows my receipts from April '75 to the same month this year to have amounted to £3,725 and I believe this is somewhere about my average income.'[12] Though any comparison of real value over time is highly risky and potentially misleading it is probably reasonable to multiply these sums by about twenty to reach a current estimate of his gross income—say £75,000 at 1975 values.[13] This is astonishing enough, but if we also take account of the changing incidence of taxation to calculate a *net* income figure we find that the equivalent gross income that he received was around half a million pounds a year in present day terms, for income tax after 1866 was levied at 4d. in the £1 (i.e. 1.67%) and in 1875 and 1876 was actually reduced to 2d. in the £1 or less than 1%.

The income that these figures represent seems scarcely credible, but there can be no doubt that Rossetti was earning more than almost any of his contemporaries no matter what their occupation. It was calculated in 1867 that the 'average' doctor might earn £300 *p.a.*, while in the same year such highly skilled and elite working-class occupations as watch-making, optical instrument making and engine driving paid an average annual wage of £91, and coal miners earned an average of £60 *p.a.*[14] In 1871 only 436 Britons were assessed for income tax under Schedule E ('salaries of employees in civil service and local government, public companies, private firms and private individuals') with incomes over £2,000 *p.a.* We may assume Rossetti was one of them.[15]

Notwithstanding this enormous income Rossetti was almost always short of cash and frequently had to sell possessions in order to tide himself over financial crises though the actual details of how he managed to spend quite so much money quite so quickly are not entirely clear.

93 *The Blue Bower* 1865

Colour 19 *The Merciless Lady* 1865

Colour 20 *The Beloved* 1865-6

In 1867, however, began a series of personal crises that were to culminate in his death fifteen years later. Essentially they took the form of a neurotic illness which began to take an increasingly severe mental and physical toll. The extent to which the symptoms were real, or were induced by persisting guilt over Lizzie Siddal's death or fears over the quality or propriety of his painting and writing, has proved a fertile field for biographical speculation.[16] The symptoms were initially insomnia and loss of vision but to these was gradually added a most extreme and ultimately devastating persecution complex which was to culminate in 1872 with a suicide attempt and a complete nervous breakdown. None of these conditions (except intermittently the insomnia) were significantly alleviated by the treatment that he took for them—chloral drops followed by neat whiskey chasers.

Around 1867-8, however, Jane Morris reappeared as a model in his painting. As *La Pia de' Tolomei* (Colour Plate 22) and again as *Mariana* (Colour Plate 23) she is used to represent a more highly developed version of what had by now become his characteristic theme. The languor, melancholy and claustrophobia of the scenes are all elements that had been present in some degree in his painting since the early 1850s, but now the formal and symbolic motifs overwhelm and dominate the composition. *La Pia* (taken from Dante's *Purgatorio*) had been locked up by her husband in a castle by the malarial swamp of Maremma where she was shortly to die. *Mariana*, though based on Shakespeare rather than Tennyson, cannot fail to evoke the lonely misery of Tennyson's poem:

> She only said 'My life is dreary— . . .
> I would that I were dead'.

The relentless gloom of these paintings is alleviated by a sensuousness and a rich, almost lurid, eroticism that greatly appealed to Rossetti's patrons. And the relationship that the paintings appeared to offer to those who bought them—the possibility of an affair (albeit cerebral) with the languid and mysterious lady whom they portrayed[17]—was in fact achieved by Rossetti, and provided him for a few years in the 1870s with the last happy period in his life. In 1871 William Morris went to Iceland for two months leaving Janey behind with Rossetti in his lovely Thames-side house at Kelmscot in Oxfordshire. The inspiration that Janey provided for the poems that he then began to write has long been used by biographers, along with various indirect references by Morris and others, to argue a more than platonic friendship, but only recently has the nature of their relationship been settled beyond any reasonable doubt.[18]

That year also saw the completion of the biggest and until then most expensive picture he had ever painted. *Dante's Dream at the Time of the Death of Beatrice* (Colour Plates 24, 25) had in fact been first conceived as long ago as 1848, and first painted in watercolour (18 in. by 26 in.) in 1856. In 1869 William Graham agreed to pay £1,575 for a version no larger than 3 ft 6 in. by 6 ft. It turned out 7 ft by 10 ft, and was eventually acquired by Liverpool Corporation direct from the artist. A comparison of the two pictures encapsulates the development of his art. Similar in general composition, Dante dreams that he is led by love, the pilgrim of the *Vita Nuova*, to see the dead Beatrice laid on a bier. Attendants lower a pall laden with symbolic mayflowers, while poppies symbolizing death litter the floor. But the simple clarity and angular expressiveness of the earlier version have been superseded by a fluent and morbid richness of colour and elaboration. The symbolism of the dying lamp, the crimson doves and the angels are new and add to the element of oppressive formalism.

Apart from his tenuous and essentially cerebral affair with Janey Morris there were few incidents in the last twenty years of Rossetti's life which had any direct bearing on his art. In one sense this is simply a reflection of the increasingly idealized and unreal nature of his pictures, but in another it is a consequence of the uneventfulness of the life itself. The menage on Cheyne Walk had its share of domestic problems—Meredith soon left, and eventually Swinburne departed too, but their place was taken by others, some genuinely friends and admirers, others mere hangers-on whose financial demands must certainly have made an impact on Rossetti's substantial income. Most notable among them was Charles Howell, an unscrupulous but colourful figure who was responsible, at Rossetti's request, for organizing in great secrecy the exhumation of Lizzie's grave in 1869 and the recovery of the manuscript of the poems that had been buried with her.

The following year they were published, along with some more recent verses, as Rossetti's first published book of poems. The reviewers were ecstatic. But many were friends of the author, and Swinburne excelled them all with thirty pages of panegyric in *The Fortnightly Review*. Eighteen months later, however, in October 1871 in the *Contemporary Review* appeared a savage though not unexpected attack by a pseudonymous Scots poet, Robert Buchanan, entitled 'The Fleshly School of Poetry: Mr. D.G. Rossetti'. Six months later it was republished, with some additions, as a pamphlet. The original robustly puritanical attack on the 'sensuality' of Rossetti's poetry was unchanged but, as William Fredeman has convincingly argued, a few

Colour 21 *Monna Vanna* 1866

Colour 22 *La Pia de' Tolomei* 1868-80

94 *Astarte Syriaca* 1877

additional passages could well have convinced the overwrought Rossetti that the exhumation of the poems and the nature of his relationship with Janey Morris were now common knowledge. Early in June 1872 the strain proved too great and Rossetti suffered a complete nervous collapse. A victim of drugs, drink and hopelessly unsatisfactory affairs, he finally succumbed to his paranoid delusions that a conspiracy had been mounted to discredit him—an ironic reversal of the real facts. Recovery was slow and in a sense never complete—for the remaining ten years of his life he became increasingly dependent on drink, drugs and friends. He quarrelled with many of the latter—Morris, Burne-Jones, and Swinburne all became estranged from him—but others took their place, and always there was the faithful and loving William to help deal with the increasingly distressing problems.

The paintings and drawings of the last ten years of his life (Plates 94-100 Colour Plates 26, 27) created in the shadow of constant illness, constant financial demands and an inevitably unsatisfactory relationship with Morris' wife, all develop the sombre features of the second version of *Dante's Dream*. Many of the drawings have a restrained sensitivity, and there is indeed something impressive about the rich elaboration of the paintings' surface detail—the endlessly convoluted and clinging foliage, the mysterious, melancholy and sometimes almost grotesque faces (nearly all in fact Mrs Morris) which 'seem to testify to some dark, unholy power, the cruelty that is akin to lust'.[20] They were rationed out by Rossetti's growing crew of helpers and hangers-on to meet an apparently insatiable demand. *Astarte Syriaca* was sold for £2,100, *Proserpine* was repeated in no less than seven additional replicas. All were extravagantly admired by their owners.

But though Rossetti constantly assured his patrons and himself that his current painting was 'as fine as anything I have done', one cannot help wondering how sincerely he felt this to be the case, and whether he was not at least in part aware of the way in which his art had been perverted by the inexorable and uncontrolled working of the market forces and his surrender to them. He was contemptuous to the last of his patrons and when from time to time he commented on his earlier work there is often a note of wistful regret which is not just a matter of old age. 'I have got the little *Annunciation*' (Colour Plate 2), he wrote to Madox Brown in 1874, 'alas! in some of the highest respects I have hardly done anything else so good. It . . . really has inspiration of the kind infectious to those born to feel it, but how many such are there? . . . Graham boggled a good deal at giving Agnew £425 for it; and as I told him, he has spent about £1,300 on absolute

Colour 24 *Dante's Dream at the Time of the Death of Beatrice* 1856

Colour 25 *Dante's Dream at the Time of the Death of Beatrice* 1871

THE BLESSED DAMOZEL

95 *The Blessed Damozel* 1875-9

96 *Jane Morris in Icelandic Costume c.* 1873

Colour 26 *Proserpine* 1877

Colour 27 *La Ghirlandata* 1873

97 *Jane Morris c.* 1873

Feb: 1873

99 *Desdemona's Death Song c.* 1878

100 Study for *The Day Dream* 1878

rubbish of mine bought here and there, which I would be only too glad to know burnt. Such is the taste even with one's best buyers.'[21]

And five years later, writing to William Graham about the status of various commissions, he voiced what now seems a pathetic plea for some kind of reassessment of his art.

I have lately again taken up the *Found* . . . the perspective and other points were difficult to manage successfully. I hope soon to be well forward in this work also. [It is] one without which I should not attempt an exhibition on account of its furnishing a refutation (I trust) to what is so often alleged against poetic painting such as I follow commonly to the best of my ability—I mean the charge that a painter adopts the poetic style simply because he cannot deal with what is real and human. I should wish to show—as such a picture as *Found* though small, must do if I succeed with it—that my preference of the ideal does not depend on incapacity to deal with simple nature.[22]

But *Found* never was finished. And though Rossetti had the capacity to deal with simple nature he lacked the will. His artistic originality was startling. He produced images of a medieval intensity, portrait sketches of astonishing insight and beauty, and finally symbolic icons whose callous, inhuman, grotesque and otherworldly power provides a strikingly ironic if accidental reflection of the forces of unfettered industrial capitalism reaching its apogee in Britain in the early 1870s. If, as I have argued, the developing crisis in late nineteenth-century art can be directly related to the uncontrolled growth of this system, and the crisis in Rossetti's art likewise, then it is a measure of his essential creative vitality that he was able even in his last years to develop a symbolic aesthetic that matched the occasion.

Notes

All books cited were first published in London unless otherwise stated.

CHAPTER 1

1. Publication dates of *Mary Barton* (1848), *Yeast* (1848), *Alton Locke* (1850) and *Sybil* (1845).
2. Publication dates of *Wives and Daughters* (1864), *The Water Babies* (1863), and *Endymion* (1880).
3. Arnold Hauser *The Social History of Art* (1962) IV, pp. 99-128 explores this change in some detail.
4. *The Prelude* Bk. XI, lines 140-44.
5. Villiers de l'Isle Adam's *Axel* (1890, trans. M. G. Rose, Dublin, 1970, p. 170). Quoted by Hauser, op. cit. p. 173, who calls it 'one of the classical portrayals of the new attitude to life, the intellectual and imaginary forms of being always stand above the rational and practical, and unrealized desires always seem more perfect than their translation into ordinary, trivial reality.'
6. For a searching and provocative examination of these theories see John Fekete 'A Theoretical Critique of Some Aspects of North American Critical Theory', unpublished Cambridge PhD Thesis, 1972. See also E. P. Thompson *William Morris* (1955) p. 28.
7. 'At a certain stage of their development, the material productive forces of society come in conflict with the existing relations of production, or—what is but a legal expression for the same thing— with the property relations within which they have been at work hitherto. From forms of development of the productive forces these relations turn into their

166

fetters. Then begins an epoch of social revolution. With the change of the economic foundation the entire immense superstructure (the legal, political, religious, aesthetic or philosophical —in short, ideological forms) is more or less rapidly transformed.' K. Marx *Preface to A Contribution to the Critique of Political Economy*. In Marx-Engels *Selected Works* (1968) pp. 181-2.

8. Derek Hudson *Munby, Man of Two Worlds* (paperback edn., 1974) p. 298. See also H. C. Marillier *D. G. Rossetti* (1899) p. 211 for a reproduction of his earliest known drawing—a rocking horse done at the age of six.

9. A friend of the exiled Kropotkin and responsible for getting Walt Whitman's *Democratic Sonnets* first published in England, his house, like his father's, became a noted gathering place for foreign revolutionists. His teenage daughters published an anarchist magazine *The Torch* and were friends of Emma Goldman, the famous American anarchist. Rossetti himself wrote a sequence of socialist sonnets. See E. Goldman *Living my Life* (New York, 1931) p. 165.

10. Quoted by Marillier op. cit. p. 7.

11. See Lionel Stevenson *The Pre-Raphaelite Poets* (Chapel Hill, N.C., 1972) pp. 24-6 for an interesting discussion of the relative pictorial values and connotations of 'My Sister's Sleep' and 'The Blessed Damozel'.

12. Now in the British Museum, it has been most recently and fully published in facsimile with transcripts and full editorial apparatus by David Erdman *The Notebook of William Blake* (Oxford, 1973).

13. See Graham Hough *The Last Romantics* (1949) p. 53.

14. O. Doughty and J. R. Wahl (eds.) *The Letters of Dante Gabriel Rossetti* 4 vols. (Oxford, 1965-7) I, p. 36 hereafter cited as *Letters*.

15. F. G. Stephens *Dante Gabriel Rossetti* (1894) p. 11.

16. March 17, 1848. Quoted by Mary Bennet *Ford Madox Brown* (exhibition catalogue, Liverpool, 1964) p. 14.

17. The sleeping figure was added later, probably in the 1860s.

18. W. Holman Hunt *Pre-Raphaelitism and the Pre-Raphaelite Brotherhood* (1905) I, p. 105.

19. W. Holman Hunt op. cit. I, p. 118.

20. E. P. Thompson op. cit. pp. 47-8.

CHAPTER 2

1. By the time he died in 1849 he had amassed a fortune of £17,000. See Dennis Farr *William Etty* (1958) p. 90.

2. See Graham Reynolds *Victorian Painters* (1966) p. 114, pl. 61.

3. See Lindsay Errington 'Social and Religious Themes in English Painting of the 1840s' unpublished PhD thesis, London University, for a fascinating examination of this picture.

4. In attention to detail and 'nature' too, Mulready anticipated many Pre-Raphaelite tenets—see Anne Rorimer *Drawings by William Mulready in the Victoria and Albert Museum* (1972) pp. 11-12.

5. It is of interest that this apparently reactionary but objectively progressive historicism should relate so directly to the work of David who played a central role in the liberation of art from its aristocratic shackles. See G. Plekhanov *Art and Social Life* (1905 trans. 1953) p. 157.

6. Quoted by Graham Reynolds op. cit. p. 34.

7. The repeal of the Corn Laws which had kept up the price of bread resulted in large scale imports of cheap foreign corn, thus reducing the rentable value of English farmland and hence impoverishing the landed aristocracy. At the same time it enabled industrialists to hold down wages, by reducing the cost of living and increasing rural pauperization, thus swelling the industrial labour force. Consequently profits and the value of industrial capital rose. The landed aristocracy never recovered from this blow.

8. Quoted from J. Ruskin *Pre-Raphaelitism* (1851) by Anne Rorimer op. cit. p. 12.

9. Quoted by Marillier op. cit. p. 22.
10. A nicely ironic example of the developing bourgeois concept of freedom. Both *exhibitor* and *visitor* in fact had to pay. The 'Freedom' consisted in the absence of any selection of exhibits, as practised by the Royal Academy.
11. *Letters* I, p. 40.
12. Ibid p. 49.
13. A reference to a peculiarly fatuous painting of anthropomorphic monkeys by Sir Edwin Landseer.
14. W. Holman Hunt op. cit. I, p. 142.
15. D. Farr op. cit. p. 133. *A Group of Captives by the Waters of Babylon.* Now in the Harris Museum and Art Gallery, Preston.
16. Diary of Ford Madox Brown in *Pre-Raphaelite Diaries and Letters*, ed. W. M. Rossetti (1900) p. 111.
17. While newly under Rossetti's spell Burne Jones wrote to a friend in 1856, 'Rossetti says some sufferings are almost necessary for a great man . . . Holman Hunt dined upon a penny a day for many years and then found it too expensive and got on with ¾d. eating sprats—for two years he never tasted meat—and Rossetti I fancy has gone through the same.' Fitzwilliam Museum, Cambridge, Burne-Jones M.S.S. Though probably true of Hunt, we may think that Rossetti was not averse to fostering misunderstandings about his own sufferings.
18. Virginia Surtees *Dante Gabriel Rossetti The Paintings and Drawings : A Catalogue Raisonée* (Oxford, 1971) p. 10. My debt to this book is enormous.
19. *Letters* I, p. 52.
20. *Letters* I, pp. 84-5.
21. See E. Halèvy *Victorian Years 1841-95* (1951) pp. 366-71. Ironically an alliance of Catholic sympathizers in the Commons with the Dissenting interest, who were reluctant to see the authority of the Church of England enhanced, contrived to emasculate the effective clause of the bill though its preamble became as a consequence even more rabidly anti-Catholic than had originally been intended.
22. Quoted by Mary Bennett *William Holman Hunt* (exhibition catalogue, 1969).
23. e.g. W. H. Deverell *Twelfth Night* (Leger Galleries, London) and C. A. Collins *The Pedlar* (City Art Gallery, Manchester).
24. *Letters* I, pp. 94-5.

CHAPTER 3

1. *Letters* I, p. 88.
2. *The Germ* I, p. 23-4. All subsequent quotations are from pp. 25-33.
3. O. Doughty *A Victorian Romantic* (1949) p. 130-1 argues fairly convincingly that the determinate ingredient was Lizzie's refusal to consummate the relationship outside wedlock, and Rossetti's reluctance to enter into the latter.
4. Quoted by Marillier op. cit. p. 38.
5. Quoted by V. Surtees op. cit. p. 189.
6. He described her thus in a letter to his sister Christina. *Letters* I, p. 109.
7. Marillier op. cit. p. 50 lists the occasions in his lifetime when Rossetti again publicly exhibited pictures. Only nine are recorded, two in Glasgow, two in Edinburgh, two in Liverpool, two in London and one in Manchester. Usually only a single picture was shown, the main exception being the great 1882 exhibition in Manchester when Rossetti allowed nine pictures to be shown. This reticence had an obvious bearing on the nature and extent of the patronage which he received.
8. *Letters* I, p. 101.
9. Ibid. pp. 122, 144.
10. Compare *Giotto Painting the Portrait of Dante* (Surtees 54) with *The First Anniversary of the Death of Beatrice* (Surtees 58).
11. Quoted by Surtees op. cit. p. 27.
12. Steven Marcus *The Other Victorians* (New York, 1966) has done much to dispel the obscurity, but the complexity and unreality of Victorian attitudes remain hard to appreciate.
13. *Letters* I, p. 72.
14. See G. P. Boyce *Diary 1851-75*

168

(Old Water Colour Society, 1941). On 16 August 1862 Boyce wrote, 'Joined Rossetti at Swinburne's rooms, where they were looking over *Justine* by the Marquis de Sade, a recent acquisition of the latter.'

In 1864 on a second visit to Paris Rossetti wrote to Swinburne that he had read the suppressed poems of Baudelaire's *Fleurs du Mal* (not allowed to be published in France till 1947) and regretted Baudelaire's absence from Paris 'or I should have met him'. *Letters* II, p. 529-30.

Arthur Munby noted in his diary on 2 December 1866 'I found Swinburne and had some talk with him about . . . Bourdelaire a certain ribald French poet whom he declared to be "15 million times better than Tennyson".' Derek Hudson ed. cit. p. 233.

15. *Dante Gabriel Rossetti : Painter and Poet* (exhibition catalogue, 1973) p. 30.
16. Quoted on the cover of the 1968 reprint of *London Labour and the London Poor* (Dover Books, New York).
17. Henry Mayhew op. cit. IV, p. 243.
18. *Letters* I, p. 331.
19. *Letters* II, p. 645.
20. Quoted by Ironside and Gere *Pre-Raphaelite Painters* (1948) p. 28. The picture is reproduced as Plate 24.
21. Quoted by Surtees op. cit. p. 27.

CHAPTER 4

1. *Letters* I, p. 357.
2. Quoted by G. H. Fleming *Rossetti and the Pre-Raphaelite Brotherhood* (1967) p. 200.
3. *Letters* I, p. 185.
4. J. Ruskin *Pre-Raphaelitism* (Everyman edition n.d.) p. 172.
5. Quoted from *The Crayon* (June 1855) by G. H. Fleming *That Ne'er Shall Meet Again* (1971) p. 64.
6. Ibid p. 65.
7. *Letters* I, p. 201, p. 245.
8. W. M. Rossetti *Dante Gabriel Rossetti : His Family Letters with a Memoir* (1885) I, p. 249-50.
9. It is interesting to note that Matthew Arnold and Swinburne himself are quoted in the Shorter Oxford English Dictionary as providing the earliest English usages of the word in this sense.
10. c.f. G. Lukacs *Writer and Critic* (1970) p. 15.
11. Quoted by G. H. Fleming *Rossetti and the Pre-Raphaelite Brotherhood* p. 103.
12. Quoted by J. E. Alden *The Pre-Raphaelites and Oxford* (Oxford, 1948) p. 36.
13. W. Holman Hunt *The Story of the Painting of the Pictures on the Walls . . . of the Old Debating Hall* (1906) p. 5.
14. Ibid. p. 14.
15. *Letters* I, p. 337.
16. W. M. Rossetti op. cit. I, p. 199.
17. Quoted by F. M. Hueffer *Ford Madox Brown* (1896) pp. 116-17.
18. G. Burne-Jones *Memorials of Edward Burne-Jones* (1904) I, p. 162.
19. E. P. Thompson, op. cit. p. 104.
20. As pointed out by Virginia Surtees, op. cit. p. 59.
21. Quoted by Fleming op cit. p. 161.
22. Boyce diary, op cit. October 13 1859.
23. Quoted by Surtees, op. cit. p. 69.
24. *Letters* I, p. 358.
25. Hall Caine *Recollections of Rossetti* (1928) p. 198-200 provides most of the evidence for the belief that she killed herself and documents Rossetti's remorse in an account of a long conversation held with him on the train from Cumberland to London a few weeks before he died.

CHAPTER 5

1. W. M. Rossetti *Some Reminiscences* (1902) p. 275.
2. Derek Hudson ed. cit. p. 297.
3. Now in the Victoria and Albert Museum. The attribution to Botticelli is not unquestioned.
4. Rossetti writing to Mrs Cowper Temple. Quoted by Surtees op. cit. p. 94.
5. F. G. Stephens op. cit. p. 52-3.
6. G. H. Fleming op. cit. p. 252.
7. *Letters* III, p. 1003.
8. The key index of this is the prices

fetched at the Plint sale in 1862: e.g. *The Wedding of St George and the Princess Sabra* (Plate 67) which Plint had bought in 1857 for 55 gns fetched £40. 19s. And *Carlisle Wall* (Colour Plate 6) fetched only £15. 4s.

9. Quoted by Surtees op. cit. p. 103.

10. It had been begun as another *Beatrice*, and the picture's details are in fact substantially at variance with the scriptural text on which it is ostensibly based.

11. Fleming op. cit. p. 254.

12. *Letters* III, p. 1435.

13. See for example the cost of living figures in E. J. Hobsbawm *Industry and Empire* (Penguin ed. 1969) Fig. 37.

14. Quoted by Geoffrey Best *Mid-Victorian Britain* (1971) pp. 90, 95-6 from R. D. Baxter *The Taxation of the UK* (1869) pp. 105-6 and Appendix IV.

15. Ibid. p. 83. This Schedule E figure is slightly misleading. Then as now real wealth was accumulated through the ownership of businesses, and profits from this were assessed under Schedule D. There were 7,500 assessments in excess of £5,000 in 1865-6 under this Schedule. Hobsbawm op. cit. p. 156.

16. See W. E. Fredeman *Prelude to the Last Decade: Dante Gabriel Rossetti in the Summer of 1872* (Manchester, 1971) for the most careful and detailed account of these crises. Fredeman makes use of much new documentation to illuminate the situation.

17. See John Berger *Ways of Seeing* (1972) pp. 45-64 and pp. 83-4.

18. See W. E. Fredeman op. cit. p. 30. He quotes a letter from William Bell Scott to Alice Boyd dated 23 October 1871. 'I told you of the second dinner party . . . well next evening I went to Morris to dinner at six. I asked Gabriel the evening before if he was to be there, and on his answering no, I said 'Why then?'. His reply was 'Oh, I have another engagement'. This engagement was actually Janey at his own home for the night! . . . Is it not too daring and altogether inexplicable?'

19. W. E. Fredeman op. cit. pp. 42-7.

20. A. C. Benson *Rossetti* (1904) p. 192.

21. *Letters* III, p. 1283.

22. *Letters* IV, p. 1635.

Index

aestheticism   18, 33, 97
Agnew's   143, 153
Allingham, William   125
anarchism   20, 167
Angelico, Fra   41, 43
Arezzo   69
aristocracy   36, 41, 67, 91, 167
Athenaeum, the   54
Axel   18, 166

Baring, Thomas   38
Bath, Marchioness of   50
Belfast   84
Birkenhead   143
Blake, William   18, 21-3, 38
   'The Chimney Sweep'   21
   'Holy Thursday'   21, 22
Botticelli, S.   41, 135
bourgeoisie   24, 36, 38, 41, 54, 94, 143
Boyce, G. P.   125, 143

Brighton   143
Browning, Robert   66-7
   Pippa Passes   66-7
Brown, Ford Madox   23-4, 25, 44,
   50, 84, 86, 91, 94, 95, 113, 153
   Work   86
   *Wycliffe Reading his Translation of
   the Bible to John of Gaunt*   23,
   24, 25, 50
Buchanan, R.   149
Burden, Jane   *see* Morris, Jane
Burne-Jones, Edward   100, 117, 153
Burne-Jones, Georgiana   100

capitalism   18, 34, 36, 40, 164, 167
Carlyle, Thomas   91
catholicism   24, 40, 51, 54, 85, 168
Cézanne, P.
   Mont Sainte Victoire   97
Chiaro dell 'Erma   69-70

Cimabue 43
Coleridge, S. T.
  'Love' 30
  'Christabel' 41
Collinson, James 48, 55
  Answering the Emigrant's Letter 54
'conservative' painting 34, 36
Contemporary Review 149
Cornforth, Fanny 125, 135
Corn Laws, repeal of 41, 167
Correggio 22
Cyclographic Club 24, 30

Dante 20, 70, 84, 148, 149
  Vita Nuova 21, 45, 149
David, J.-L. 40
Deverell, Walter 70, 91
  The Irish Vagrants 91
Dickens, Charles 38
Diderot, D. 97
Disraeli, Benjamin 17
Dunn, H. Treffry 91
  *Rossetti's Sitting Room at 16,
    Cheyne Walk* 140
Durer, A. 91
Durham, Bishop of 54
Dyce, William 41, 43, 55
  Christabel 41, 42
  Virgin and Child 42

Ecclesiastical Titles Bill 54
Egg, Augustus 55
Eliot, George 17
Elmore, Alfred 36, 38
  The Origin of the Stocking Frame
    36-38
  The Invention of the Combing Loom
    38
Etty, William 34, 36, 50
  The Judgement of Paris 34, 35

Fenians 91
Ferdinand, King of Naples 20
Fleming, G. H. 144
Fortnightly Review 149
Foscolo 20
Fredeman, William 149
'Free Exhibition' 23, 45, 168

Gambart, E. 143
Gaskell, Elizabeth 17, 91
  Mary Barton 91
Germ, The 67

Gilbert, John 30
Gillott, J. 50
Giotto 38, 43
Glasgow 95
Goethe, J. W. 97
  Faust 30
Gothic 38, 40
Graham, William 94-5, 143, 149, 153

Harvard 113
Holy Land 55
Howell, Charles 149
Hughes, Arthur 100, 125
Hunt, William 'Bird's Nest' 43
Hunt, William Holman 23, 24, 33,
  40, 43, 44, 48-58, 70, 84, 86, 125
  The Awakening Conscience 86
  *A Converted British Family
    Sheltering a Christian Priest from
    the Persecution of the Druids* 54
  The Eve of St Agnes 24, 27, 33
  *Valentine Rescuing Sylvia from
    Proteus* 58, 59
Huysmans, J. K.
  A Rebours 69
Iceland 148
Ingres, J. A. D. 40, 48
Ireland 36, 91
Isle, Ambrose Phillips de l' 40

Jamesone, Mrs 41
  Poetry of Sacred and Legendary Art
    40

Keats, John 21, 33, 40, 45
Kingsley, Charles 17, 41
Knole Park, Sevenoaks 55

Landseer, Sir Edwin 34, 36
Leathart 94
Leeds 38
Lessing 97
Lewis, J. F. 43
Leyland 143
Lindsay
  *Sketches of the History of Christian
    Art* 40
Liverpool 143, 149
Llandaff, cathedral 66, 119
London
  Blackfriars Bridge 77, 134
  Charlotte Street 20
  Cheyne Walk 134-5, 140

Green Park 86
Hyde Park 86
King's College School 20
Leicester Square 70
Mall, the 86
National Gallery 51
North London Drawing School,
    Hampstead 50
Parliament, Houses of 40, 41
Royal Academy 24, 38, 55
Royal Academy Schools 20, 23,
    24, 44, 48

MacCracken, Francis 84, 94
Malory 84, 100, 105, 113
    Morte d'Arthur 100
Manchester 91
Marks, Murray 135
Marx, Karl 18
Mayhew, Henry 86, 91
    London Labour and the London Poor
    86, 91
Mazzini 20
Memling, H. 51
Meredith, George 134, 149
Michelangelo 48
Middle class *see* bourgeoisie
Millais, John Everett 33, 40, 43, 48,
    50-5, 96
    Christ in the House of his Parents 54
Morris, Jane 85, 105, 113, 148-9,
    153, 170
Morris, William 100, 105, 117, 119,
    148, 153
    Queen Guinevere 112, 113
    The Defence of Guinevere 113
        'The Blue Closet' 113
        'The Defence of Guinevere' 119
        'The Haystack in the Floods'
        113, 117, 119
        'Sir Peter Harpdon's End' 117
        'The Tune of Seven Towers' 113
Morris & Co. 127
Mulready, William 38, 41, 43
    The Sonnet 38, 39
    *Train up a Child the way he should
        go* 38
Munby, A. 135

Naples 20
Nazarenes 23, 40, 41
Newcastle 94
Norton, Charles Eliot 113

Orcagna 40, 43, 48
Oxford
    University Union 100, 105

Palmer, Samuel 21
Palmer, William 21
'Papal Aggression, the' 54
Pater, W. 97
patronage 36, 38, 55, 84-5, 91, 93,
    94-7, 143, 144, 153, 164
Pisa 69
    Campo Santo 40, 48
    San Rocco 69
Pisano brothers 69
Poe, Edgar Allen 30, 32, 33
Polidori, Frances 20
Pollen, Hungerford 100
Pre-Raphaelite Brotherhood 23, 33,
    36, 38, 40, 45, 48-58, 70, 95, 119
prices 50, 94, 96, 119, 143, 144, 153,
    164, 169-70
Primitifs, les 40
Prinsep, Val 100, 117
'progressive' painting 34, 41, 43
prostitution 85-6, 91, 94
Pugin, A. W. N. 40

Quay, Maurice 40
radicalism 20
Rae, G. 143, 144
Raphael 38, 43, 45, 48
realism 23, 33, 43-4, 45, 58, 113, 164
Redgrave, Richard
    The Poor Teacher 37, 38
Rembrandt 22
revolution 20, 24, 48, 97
Reynolds, Sir Joshua 22, 34
    Discourses on Art 22
Rio
    Poésie de l'art Chrétien 40
romanticism 21, 33, 119
Rossetti, Christina 45, 48, 51
Rossetti, Dante Gabriel
    art, view of 22-3, 43-4, 58, 97, 164
    draughtsmanship 30
    education 20-4
    financial position 50, 84, 119, 134,
        144, 168
    'Hand and Soul' 67
    health 148, 153
    poetry 21, 113
        'The Blessed Damozel' 21
        'Jenny' 85-6, 93

'My Sister's Sleep' 21
The New Life 21, 45
visits to France and Belgium 51,
  85, 169
see also patronage, prices, technique,
  subject matter
Algernon Charles Swinburne 101
*Angels Watching over the Crown of
  Thorns* 24, 26
The Annunciation 65, 66
  see also Ecce Ancilla Domini!
Arthur's Tomb 98, 105
Astarte Syriaca 18, 152, 153
The Attainment of the Sanc Grael
  105, 108
The Ballad of Fair Annie 83
Beata Beatrix 70, 111, 135, 143
*Beatrice Meeting Dante at a
  Wedding Feast Denies him her
  Salutation* 97
Before the Battle 106, 113
The Beloved 143, 147
The Blessed Damozel 156
The Blue Bower 143, 144, 145
The Blue Closet 113, 114
Bocca Baciata 124, 125, 135, 143
Bottles 24, 26
The Bower Meadow 58, 59
Carlisle Wall 60
Cassandra 127, 128
The Chapel before the Lists 102, 113
A Christmas Carol 113, 116
*D. G. Rossetti Sitting to Elizabeth
  Siddal* 80
The Damsel of the Sanct Grael 71,
  113
Dante's Dream 45, 149, 153, 155
*Dante Interrupted while Drawing an
  Angel on the Anniversary of
  Beatrice's Death* 45, 46, 47,
  48-9, 83
Dante's Vision of Rachel and Leah
  61, 66
The Day Dream 163
Death of a Wombat 140
The Death of Breuze sans Pitié 113
Desdemona's Death Song 162
Dr Johnson at the Mitre 127, 128
Ecce Ancilla Domini! (The
  Annunciation) 51, 52, 54, 66,
  67, 84, 85, 119, 153
Elizabeth Siddal 72-9
Fair Rosamund 135, 141

Fanny Cornforth 136
*Faust — Gretchen and
  Mephistopheles in the Church* 28,
  29, 30, 45
A Fight for a Woman 142, 143
The First Madness of Ophelia 127,
  131
Ford Madox Brown 25
Found 18, 64, 85-91, 94, 164
Gabriele Rossetti 19
The Gate of Memory 92-3
Genevieve 30, 31, 33, 45
The Girlhood of Mary Virgin 18,
  24, 44-5, 49, 50, 51, 119
A Girl Singing to a Lute 56
Hamlet and Ophelia 127, 130, 133
Helen of Troy 135
Hesterna Rosa 91-3
'Hist' said Kate the Queen 66-8
*How Sir Galahad, Sir Bors and
  Sir Percival were fed with the
  Sanc Grael, but Sir Percival's
  sister Died by the Way* 99, 105
How They Met Themselves 127, 130
Jane Morris 105, 109, 160-1
Jane Morris in Icelandic Costume
  157
La Belle Dame sans Merci 83
The Laboratory 67, 68
La Ghirlandata 159
La Pia de 'Tolomei 148, 151
Mariana 148, 154
Mary in the House of St John 63,
  66, 85
*Mary Magdalene at the Door of
  Simon the Pharisee* 119, 123
The Merciless Lady 143, 146
Monna Vanna 144, 150
Morning Music 138
Paolo and Francesca 82
The Passover in the Holy Family
  62, 66
Proserpine 153, 158
The Quest of the Holy Grail 57, 77
The Raven 32
Ruth and Boaz 53, 66
St Catherine 103, 113
St Cecilia 81
St George and the Dragon 126
St John Comforting the Virgin 65,
  66
The Seed of David 66, 110, 118-21,
  143

Self Portrait   19, 20
Sir Galahad at the Ruined Chapel
   107, 113
Sir Launcelot in the Queen's Chamber
   119, 122
*Sir Launcelot's Vision of the Sanc
   Grael*   98, 104, 105
The Sleeper   32
The Tune of Seven Towers   99, 113
Ululame   32
The Wedding of St George   126
*The Wedding of St George and the
   Princess Sabra*   113, 115
Woman Combing her Hair   137
Woman with a Fan   139
Writing on the Sand   127, 129
Rossetti, Gabriele   19, 20
Rossetti, William Michael   20, 45,
   48, 55, 67, 96, 105, 134, 153
Rossini, Giacomo   20
Rousseau, J. J.   97
Rubens, P. P.   22
Ruskin, John   41, 43-4, 95, 96, 97,
   100, 105
   Modern Painters   43, 44
Russell, Lord John   54

Scott, Walter   20
Scott, William Bell   86, 127
   'Rosabell'   86
sexism   36, 93
Shakespeare, William   20, 148
Sheepshanks, John   38
Shelley, Percy Bysshe   18
Siddal, Elizabeth   21, 70-84, 85, 105,
   113, 127, 132, 134, 135, 148, 149
   Clerk Sanders   80
   The Quest of the Holy Grail   57, 77
socialism   20, 167
Song of Solomon   144
Stanhope, Spencer   125
Stephens, F. G.   48, 100, 143
subject matter   66-7, 69-70, 77,
   84-5, 94, 113, 125, 126, 143, 164
Surtees, Virginia   86
Swinburne, A. C.   91, 97, 100, 101,
   134, 149, 153, 169

Taylor, Henry
   Philip van Artevelde   93
technique   23, 36, 38, 41, 43, 45, 50,
   51, 77, 91, 113, 119, 125, 126, 153,
   164

Temple, William Cowper   143
Tennyson, A.   148
Thackeray, William   17, 86
Thompson, E. P.   117
Trinity House   55
Trist   143
Trollope, Anthony   17
Tupper, Jack   58
Turner, J. M. W.   36, 96, 97
   Norham Castle   97
   Rain, Steam and Speed   36

Van Eyck   51

Whistler, James McNeil   135
Wilkie, Sir David   34, 36
   The Irish Whiskey Still   35
Woodward   100
Woolner, Thomas   48, 55
Wordsworth, William   18, 33
   Prelude   18
working class   24, 54, 67, 91
Wright, Joseph, of Derby   36
Wycliffe, John   24

Yeats, W. B.   18